POLICING
FERGUSON
POLICING
AMERICA

POLICING
FERGUSON

POLICING
AMERICA

WHAT REALLY HAPPENED—AND WHAT
THE COUNTRY CAN LEARN FROM IT

THOMAS JACKSON
FORMER POLICE CHIEF OF
FERGUSON, MISSOURI

Skyhorse Publishing

Skyhorse Publishing books may be purchased in bulk at special discounts for sales promotion, corporate gifts, fund-raising, or educational purposes. Special editions can also be created to specifications. For details, contact the Special Sales Department, Skyhorse Publishing, 307 West 36th Street, 11th Floor, New York, NY 10018 or info@skyhorsepublishing.com.

Skyhorse® and Skyhorse Publishing® are registered trademarks of Skyhorse Publishing, Inc.®, a Delaware corporation.

Visit our website at www.skyhorsepublishing.com.

10 9 8 7 6 5 4 3 2

Library of Congress Cataloging-in-Publication Data is available on file.

Cover design by Brian Peterson
Cover photo credit: Steve Pellegrino
Interior photos: Steve Pellegrino

Print ISBN: 978-1-5107-1976-7
Ebook ISBN: 978-1-5107-1977-4

Printed in the United States of America

This book is dedicated to the thin blue line,
which remains unbroken.

Contents

Preface

The name of Ferguson, Missouri, means a lot of different things to different people. To me, it means home. It's where I staked my life and my livelihood.

My father moved our family from my boyhood home in Pittsfield, Massachusetts, in 1966 to take a job as an electrical engineer at Emerson Electric Company in Ferguson. He and my mother also owned a paint and crafts shop (one block from the police station) where I worked when I was in high school.

So much of what people believe about what happened in Ferguson, and about the town and its people, is completely untrue, thanks to the news media, the internet, and a deeply flawed government examination. Still, some of the larger issues that Ferguson has come to represent are real, and of critical importance to the future of the country. I do hope to set the record straight, not just about the shooting and the police response to it, but about what America can and should expect from its law enforcement professionals. What was considered a noble, maybe even heroic, calling only a few years ago became the perceived source of all of America's woes practically overnight.

In writing this book, I hope to do my part in restoring the public trust to police, but I don't want the discussion about policing to continue to serve as a distraction from more basic social concerns. Failing programs that get in the way of the very benefits they were intended to provide have created a cycle of poverty and stagnation that law enforcement deals with every day. I hope to share my experience in a way that opens that conversation and starts us on a path toward police—all citizens, in fact—playing a more proactive role in improving the lives of all Americans.

Introduction

In August 2014, on a hot Saturday afternoon in Missouri, Officer Darren Wilson of the Ferguson Police Department shot and killed Michael Brown. America was transfixed for months by the protests, the riots, the never-ending news cycle. What was considered a noble, even heroic calling—police work—came to be perceived as the source of America's woes practically overnight. The name of Ferguson became shorthand for institutional racism and police brutality.

I was the chief of police for Ferguson. The incident that resulted in the death of Michael Brown, and the terrible aftermath that all but destroyed the town, happened on my watch.

I spent months on the hot seat, the primary focus of a nation's outrage. It was probably more important to me than to anyone else to understand where that anger came from, to realistically assess how much of it was justified, and how much resulted from people jumping to conclusions based on a dangerous cocktail of provocative media reports and inflammatory pronouncements by politicians and activists, amplifying misperceptions that had spread on the internet faster than any investigation could possibly proceed.

Since resigning my post, in the wake of the US Department of Justice's scathing report, I've had the time and motivation to examine all the things said about Ferguson. Even if there weren't lawsuits that required me to be clear about the facts, I needed to know for my own peace of mind where people came up with the claims they made about my force and our town. As a professional, I wanted to know what we were doing wrong and how to fix what could be fixed, even if my days as chief in Ferguson were over.

This book is a product of that examination.

I cannot begin without first addressing two things: the Department of Justice report on Ferguson and the fact that there was so much coverage of events in Ferguson that people say, "I know what I saw. You can't deny it."

You know what you saw. There's a difference between, "I know what I saw," and "I know what I was shown." Even if you came to Ferguson to see with your own eyes, there were places you couldn't have gone, meetings you couldn't have attended. All I ask is that you give me a chance to show you what wasn't shown, to take you where you couldn't have gone.

The DOJ report, though, needs to be discussed right here, right off the bat.

Attorney General Eric Holder of the Department of Justice first arrived in Ferguson eleven days after the shooting. He spoke with Michael Brown's mother. He talked of his own experiences with prejudice. He stated publicly that his pledge included, as opposed to simple justice, "robust action," and he stated that "long after the events of August 9 have receded from the headlines, the Justice Department will continue to stand with this community." The things he said and did added up to a tacit confirmation of the public fear that wrong had been done, the shooting had been bad, and that prejudice was a factor. And it was all broadcast live. It not only cemented the Department of Justice's biased stance in the upcoming investigation but also turned up the heat of public anger. He made the job of law enforcement even harder than it already was, putting the public and police both at greater risk.

Attorney General Holder did all of this more than *three months* before the investigation into the shooting concluded. *Three months* before the facts were in. His mind was made up before he arrived in town. Following his August 20 pledge and his September resignation, Holder appeared at the Washington Ideas Forum on October 29, where he declared, "I think it's pretty clear that the need for wholesale change in that department [Ferguson] is appropriate."

The *Los Angeles Times* later quoted sources in the Justice Department saying, "The more he gets out in front publicly, the more he will be expected to deliver criminal charges . . . the situation could reach a tipping point where federal criminal charges would be the only way to vindicate Holder's public comments."

Then the investigations into the shooting concluded and the forensics showed that the narrative that had gained such traction with the public didn't fit the evidence. The officer's version of events did. To those who right here would immediately jump to thinking "staged scene, cover-up," I have included an appendix so you can read the findings yourself. Mind you, what I've included is not from an internal police investigation—it's from a federal investigation, because the FBI (a division of the DOJ) was sent to look into this at the same time that Holder was sent.

The FBI came, stayed off camera, and did their jobs. They actually investigated before reaching their conclusions. They brought in the evidence, and it supported the police officer whom Holder had tacitly condemned.

It's one thing for a shopkeeper to say, "I might have made an unfair rush to judgment here," and quite another for the attorney general of the United States to say, "Oops."

What are the odds of a fair and unbiased investigation if the person directing it is thoroughly invested in finding something that will vindicate *him* rather than in finding the truth? The DOJ investigation started with the premise that Ferguson was a swamp of injustice, then sought out and published anything that looked like it supported that position.

I don't want to imply the department I led was immaculate, that no Ferguson officer ever engaged in questionable behavior, and I don't deny that there are systemic problems or that the criminal justice system is in need of lasting reform. But the Ferguson portrayed in that report was an invention, a backwards, angry place that the Justice Department created to make a show of tearing it down.

Seven months after the shooting and three months after the grand jury had ruled that there were no grounds to indict the officer involved, I was summoned to meet with representatives of the DOJ prior to the report's release. As the city's manager, attorney, mayor, and I went into the meeting, we were required to surrender cell phones and recording devices, as if they didn't want anybody to know what they were about to say.

We listened in horror as the DOJ lead investigator outlined the essential findings in the report. A stunned

Stephanie Karr, our city attorney, protested, "You can't say those things. That's not true. It won't hold up in litigation."

The DOJ investigator replied coldly, "Well, we aren't litigating, are we?"

In the court of public opinion, there is no standard of proof, much less a defense team. We knew their report was a distorted misrepresentation, but they counted on the public not to question it. By the time sources like the *Wall Street Journal* condemned them for the meaningless way they used statistics, for example, it was too late. The damage was done.

I still shake my head over how easily they could publish a report filled with so much that met no evidentiary standards simply by playing to what "everybody knew."

Everybody knew. How quickly a few social media reports grew into "everybody knows."

It was like a chain reaction that got out of control. Social media sources and traditional media sources were feeding off each other. The crowds were responding to what the police were doing. The more it escalated, the more people showed up, and the more people showed up, the more it escalated. It was a toxic feedback loop.

My grim observation in Ferguson was that media representatives and politicians, whose careers depend on keeping in favor with the public, let themselves be swept up by the viral version. They lost objectivity. They did not wait for the facts.

True justice stands upon the facts, no matter how much they fly in the face of popular perception. True justice is impartial, and for everyone.

Justice, for some, is an eye for an eye, a life for a life. It means doing unto others as they have done unto you. But that's not justice; that's vengeance. Vengeance wants to inflict pain on another because pain was inflicted on you.

That doesn't remove the pain. It doubles the pain, and is especially harmful if the pain is inflicted on those who never deserved it, as in Ferguson.

A desire for vengeance comes from anger, frustration, and passion. It has destruction as a goal, destruction of what was wrong, but it extends to anything else the anger turns upon as well.

A desire for true justice comes from reason, and it holds out hope. The foundation of justice must rest upon the truth, in all its complexity, to build something new.

Chapter 1

Officer-Involved
Fatal Shooting

In August 2014, I was serving as chief of police in Ferguson, Missouri (population about 21,000). It sounds like a small town, and to many across the country just saying "Missouri" conjures rural imagery.

In fact, Ferguson is one of about ninety municipalities in St. Louis County. The nearby City of St. Louis is its own county, with its own government. The MetroLink rail and MetroBus systems connect and serve both the city and county within the greater metropolitan area. About two-thirds of the municipalities, like Ferguson, have their own police departments; some combine resources, and some contract with St. Louis County. Some areas are unincorporated and rely solely on St. Louis County for services. Some, like Ferguson, are served by their own fire departments, others are served by fire districts, and a few have a mixture of the two, thanks to annexations over the years. School districts, like fire districts, are their own taxing bodies, independent of local governments, and often cross municipal lines. Ferguson is served by two different school districts.

From Ferguson, drive twenty minutes one direction and you're in downtown St. Louis City at the Arch; go ten minutes the other direction and you're at the airport. In the middle of urban sprawl, Ferguson contains everything from apartments and starter homes to mansions, local shops to major chain stores, and small businesses to one of the Fortune 500. The city boasts eleven parks, an aquatic center and a community center, nineteen churches, great places to eat, an organic apprenticeship farm and thriving farmers' market, and one of three area-wide community colleges. A sign welcomes you to Historic Ferguson, its motto: Proud Past, Promising Future. It has been designated a Playful City USA community and an Arbor Day Foundation Tree City USA.

I had been chief in Ferguson since 2010, and a cop for thirty-five years. My first thirty-one years were with the St. Louis County Police Department, where I retired as a captain. I came to police work after a stint as a paramedic, because being an EMT made me feel like I was always getting involved in situations after the damage was done. I didn't want to just pick up the victims; I wanted to be in a position to prevent people from becoming victims in the first place.

August 9, 2014, was my day off, and I was a distance from town when I received a chilling call. There had been an officer-involved fatal shooting on Canfield Drive near the intersection of West Florissant Avenue. That put the shooting in the middle of an area containing many federally subsidized housing units.

In the years before I became police chief, the number of public housing units there had grown very quickly along Canfield and Northwinds Estates Drives. The residents made up a significant percentage of the town's population.

2

Most of the residents were low-income, many working multiple low-wage jobs to try to provide for their families, and many were on some form of public assistance. I had seen right away, from assessing our crime statistics, that they were dealing with the highest concentration of both petty crimes and more serious, sometimes violent crimes in their neighborhoods.

When I first came on the job in Ferguson, many of the public apartment complexes were physically falling apart, largely ignored by inattentive management companies working for absentee landlords who just sat back and collected federal subsidies. Over time, we tracked down the owners of all the buildings, some living as far away as Massachusetts, and, one by one, got them to enter into agreements with the city to clean up their properties.

This went beyond long-neglected maintenance and repairs and called on the owners to improve the quality of life in other ways. We asked the owners to issue vehicle parking stickers, provide security guards and cameras throughout the apartment complexes, and enforce occupancy and safety codes. The process of installing the security cameras was underway in the area, and that August it was about two weeks from completion.

This didn't address the real underlying problem of concentrated poverty, but at the very least, it was one step toward making these neighborhoods more livable. I'm sure there were any number of local, state, and federal agencies better equipped, better trained, and with sufficient resources to improve the state of housing for their residents, but in their absence, we, local law enforcement, were the ones there, feet on the ground. So we sponsored job fairs and volunteer programs, and established community resource officers (CROs), to help businesses and neighborhoods identify and resolve problems. We partnered with the school district to provide school resource officers (SROs) to establish rapport with students, teach the D.A.R.E. (Drug Abuse Resistance Education) program, and give teachers a point of contact with the police department. We helped the residents establish neighborhood watch associations. I served on commissions trying to attract new businesses to bring new jobs to the area and worked with the municipal court to arrange public-service sentencing alternatives, expunging fines and creating amnesty programs.

I urged my officers to be a presence in the neighborhood, getting to know people, off duty as well as on the job. I can't even count the number of ball games, church picnics, block parties, and fairs that either I or one of my officers attended. We had been in the Canfield Green Apartments not long before, out of uniform, handing out flyers urging residents to attend the grand opening of our new community center.

The city had undertaken these efforts on its own initiative to improve trust and quality of life, but there is a high changeover rate in public housing, and new people would come in unfamiliar with us and our efforts. We were working constantly to improve trust, but the police can gain only so much traction in the face of poverty, governmental mismanagement, and cultural predisposition. Still, we came to the community the same way we had come to the job—to do what could be done.

When the call came in on that hot August day, and the veteran sergeant on the phone said, "It's getting ugly here" of an incident that was only minutes old, I felt like a societal EMT, dealing with the consequences because I could not address the true causes. I turned my car back toward Ferguson to put on my uniform and do my job. But in this case, part of my job was handing the investigation over to someone else.

My first call was to Dan DeCarli, chief of detectives on the Ferguson force. Dan was a seasoned investigator and the commander of the Major Case Squad of Greater St. Louis, which is composed of detectives from various departments and responds to unsolved homicides area-wide as needed or requested. DeCarli already had his team from Ferguson on the way out to start working the scene. I told Dan that I felt it would be prudent to turn the investigation of the shooting over to another law enforcement agency, in this case, the St. Louis County Police Department. He agreed that our professional and capable detectives would not conduct the investigation, to avoid any appearance of impropriety. I phoned Chief Jon Belmar of the county police and laid out the situation. Belmar assured me he would immediately take over the investigation and also have his people take over the scene of the shooting. Jon and I had worked together for years, and I had complete confidence that he would do his job and do it well. He would make certain his detectives were on the case and would make a fair report of all that had happened—for me, for the town of Ferguson, and for the public.

Assured that the situation was now in good, capable hands, I hung up, stopped to change out of my weekend clothes into uniform, and drove to the scene. I knew it was going to be a long and difficult day; but no one could have known that the day would stretch to six months and would change the lives of so many people, that it would tear our town apart, and that it would alter the feelings of the entire country.

By the time I got to Canfield, forty-five minutes after the shooting, a crowd of perhaps two hundred people had already gathered, and officers were busy establishing a boundary around the area with yellow police tape. The young man's body—Michael Brown, as I would soon learn—lay on the ground just inside the Canfield apartment complex, not visible from West Florissant Avenue, the main road. Some way down the street, a police car was parked at a crooked angle, as if in haste, with the driver's door open. The sergeant told me that an ambulance had already come and gone. While the EMTs were able to pronounce Michael Brown dead at the scene, they could not remove his body before the crime scene investigation team arrived, collected physical evidence, and thoroughly documented the scene. We didn't know then that the team was currently wrapping up their work following a hostage crisis nearly an hour away, and that the time Brown's body would remain there for all to see would stretch on for hours.

For the first hour, everything seemed to be stuck in neutral. While we waited for the crime scene investigators, Jon Belmar's detectives did the best they could to scour and secure the scene. As time passed, the tension and anger in the crowd steadily grew more palpable. This officer-involved shooting had taken place at approximately noon, in full view of people on the street and in the surrounding apartment buildings, and had immediately caught the attention of everybody in the neighborhood. Smartphones armed with Twitter, Instagram, Facebook, and messaging apps had sent out news of the shooting within minutes, bringing even more onlookers. Fueled by social media, a narrative had already begun to take shape, even before the press, local authorities, or adequate police arrived. An initial posting online, on Twitter, read, "Ferguson police just executed an unarmed 17yr old boy that was walking to the store. Shot him 10 times smh [shaking my head]." Before anybody knew any specifics about the shooting, that narrative immediately cast the Ferguson police as the wrongdoers. Taunts and curses such as "Fuck the police!" and "Killer cops!" as well as shouts for "Justice now!" filled the air.

As the crowd and the hostility grew, the county captain called what's known as a "Code 1000," a kind of all-hands-on-deck for assistance that goes out to all the local law enforcement agencies. I had used this call for assistance in Ferguson in the wake of tornados in 2011 and 2013. We felt a sense of foreboding, as if the crowd were closing in, and could erupt into mayhem at any moment.

The Ferguson lieutenant on the scene was Bill Ballard, a plain-spoken, tough former Marine drill sergeant. "Well, Chief," he said, "this went to shit pretty quick."

That about summed it up.

"None of this looks good." That was the assessment of Anthony Shahid, an activist in African American issues well known around St. Louis. I saw him standing in the crowd shortly after I arrived and reached out for his help to ease the crowd's nerves and tension. Anthony and I walked the line of police tape around the perimeter of the scene, imploring crowds to stay back and remain calm, and to let the police do their job.

At Shahid's suggestion, we also enlisted the help of Lesley McSpadden, Michael Brown's mother, who had arrived at the scene. I had never met her, or Michael, or anyone in the family before that day out on Canfield Drive, nor would I have any direct contact with her after that, but her presence there, with Shahid and me, helped to keep the tension from boiling over. I don't know that I could have accomplished that on my own. Most people in Ferguson knew me and my officers, many of whom had served Ferguson for decades, and we had strong ties to every part of the community. But in that moment, in that simmering crowd, they saw only police, and police were already perceived to be the bad guys.

As the three of us were talking and walking along the perimeter, my cell phone rang. John Shaw, the charismatic young city manager of Ferguson, sounded uncharacteristically grim. John was a top-notch city manager, well respected in his profession and by his colleagues. "Chief, I need you to deal with the news people on the scene!" he said. He wanted me to try to "head off" the bad press that had already begun to circulate about the shooting. Already? I don't think either of us understood that ship had sailed. I had only just begun to notice television trucks arriving and reporters with microphones or notepads wading through the crowd. None of us had had a chance to stop and think how many of the people on the street that day had smartphones with them, and how many had immediately started to circulate text messages, tweets, retweets, hashtags, Facebook posts, or Instagram images.

It's important to understand that Canfield Drive and West Florissant Avenue are the main drags of this particular section of Ferguson. The corner where they come together is a central hub in the community and always busy with cars passing through, pedestrians strolling, and people shopping at a number of stores within a hundred yards in any direction. There were always a few people just hanging out. It was as if Michael Brown had been shot in the town square at high noon. It would take months for the county, the FBI, and the United States Department of Justice to sort out the dozens of people who claimed to be witnesses and determine their reliability, but the flood of social media posts was never subjected to that kind of scrutiny, nor were the live television interviews that avid reporters broadcast from the scene. Rumors spread through the crowd like wildfire, and took off at an even faster rate through the internet. The rumors, exaggerations, and other misinformation in all those messages became the fuel for the coming firestorm.

Things didn't stay calm for very long. I was as surprised as anyone else out there to see a team of officers with police dogs suddenly rush into the crowd. Ferguson Canine Officer Greg Casem was already present with his four-legged partner, which at the time was sitting calmly by his side as Greg spoke to members of the crowd. When the county captain realized that the gathering crowds were growing agitated, he had called in for additional canines. It made sense at the time, but the appearance of the new dogs enraged the crowd, bringing back images of Selma. Seeing the problems created by the mere presence of the dogs, the county captain quickly ordered them withdrawn, but the damage had been done. Whatever progress we might have made in settling the crowd suddenly meant nothing.

It felt as if so many aspects of the day were developing all at the same time. About two hours into the situation, a number of critical things happened. First, a reporter recorded and broadcast an interview from the street with Dorian Johnson, the young man who had been with Michael Brown at the time of the encounter with Officer Darren Wilson. It was Johnson who first put forth the story that Brown had tried to surrender peacefully, that he had his hands in the air, asking Wilson not to shoot. Although county prosecutor Bob McCulloch and the FBI later determined that nothing of the kind had happened, and that Johnson had not been in a position to actually see the shooting, his false description became the narrative, a narrative that went on to define a social movement. Standing in the middle of a hostile mob that day, I had no idea that the world had already latched on to this tale. I wouldn't learn about it until much later when I saw Johnson's interview on CNN.

This new media dynamic—the intersection of traditional journalism and spontaneous reporting via the internet and social media—became apparent from the start, and would continue to be one of the most significant themes of the entire experience.

At about the same time, the sound of gunfire filled the air. Nobody knows for sure how many shots were fired—maybe three, or four, or even five—but the effect on the already simmering crowd and the hyper-alert law enforcement presence was frightening. Gunfire erupted again from the back of the crowd to the east at least two more times that I can remember. Police were never able to identify the source of the gunshots, but the tension felt like it could explode into a riot at any moment.

Jon Belmar's crime scene investigation team entered into this highly charged atmosphere. The job of collecting physical evidence and interviewing witnesses is difficult enough under any circumstances. I have no doubt that every investigator and officer on the scene that Saturday felt the eyes of a suspicious public on them as they focused on doing a painstakingly thorough job in a crime scene that certainly already had been contaminated.

When crime scene investigators put a privacy barrier around the body, Anthony Shahid approached me and said that some of the crowd were thinking it was done so we could plant a gun. I asked him to stand with me while that area was processed, which seemed to satisfy the skeptics.

One colleague I sent away from the scene was my newly appointed assistant chief, Al Eickhoff. Al and I knew each other throughout our careers, having been awarded the Medal of Valor together years before when we were both members of the St. Louis County SWAT Unit. I had only recently brought him into the department. That hot Saturday was a kind of brutal welcome to Ferguson for him. I asked Al to return to the police station and keep an eye on Darren Wilson, who needed to be treated for injuries to his face, and to be questioned by the county police investigators.

Eventually, the crime scene team wrapped up its investigation. Four hours after he had died, Michael Brown's body was placed in a coroner's vehicle and removed. The law enforcement people began to disassemble the crime scene, taking down and rolling up the yellow police tape and gradually reducing the very large police presence. I remember thinking—or maybe, hoping—that the crowds would start to disperse, that people would go home to their families and neighborhoods, that the police could dig quickly into their investigations, and that the city could begin to process and understand, and ultimately move past this horrible day. I've never been so wrong about anything in my life.

When I look back now over those first few hours, I see so many things that occurred—some large, some small—that contributed to the storm of rage and misunderstanding that continued for at least six more months, and that would become essential parts of the narrative. Every step I took and every decision I made that afternoon was by the book. I followed procedures and protocols designed to ensure the fairness and transparency of investigations. I made the safety and security of the public my chief concern, as did every commander and officer at the scene. And yet, nearly every one of those moves backfired in some way. Whatever we did, it seemed, was to be misinterpreted or misconstrued to make a social or political point. I'm not saying that the point didn't need to be made. I'm saying that it had little or nothing to do with the facts surrounding Darren Wilson's shooting of Michael Brown.

11

Even the smallest and, to me, most clear-cut decisions I made on that first afternoon would come back to haunt me. Right away, I turned the investigation over to another law enforcement body, taking the matter completely out of my hands and out of the hands of the Ferguson force. When Jon Belmar assured me he had the situation covered, I took it to mean nothing more than that he would do his job. He's a smart, experienced, and well-trained professional, and I could depend on the people under him to take their work seriously and deliver a fair report to me and to the community. He also had been a friend and colleague for many years. I was one of his mentors when we served on the SWAT team, and I had retired as a captain from the police department he now headed. It never crossed my mind that others would view Belmar's participation suspiciously: police investigating other police, perhaps a simple case of good friends watching each other's backs.

The fact is that I had worked my entire career in the St. Louis area. I knew people throughout the local, county, and state agencies, and even a number of federal officials. Of course I was familiar with many of the law enforcement people on the scene that day, but never for a moment did I think that had any impact on the professionalism of the investigation. Still, from the taunts and jeers on the street as the investigators worked, it was clear that the onlookers assumed from the start that some kind of cover-up had already begun. Nobody in that crowd trusted the officers to carry out a righteous investigation.

This was to be one of the many hard lessons I learned that day in what people call "optics." Optics: not how things *are*, just how things *look*. Basically, it became clear to me over the next few months that more often than not, questions of right and wrong are not as important as how things look.

You may do the right thing, and for all the right reasons, and it will still be wrong because it might appear wrong in some people's eyes.

Next—and if I had it to do over again, this is where I might have questioned inflexible protocol—Michael Brown's body would not have lain in the street for four hours. Anybody who has watched a police drama on television knows that you don't move a body at a crime scene until the forensics team has examined both the body and the scene in detail. Moving the body can cause lost or tainted evidence, and even in a case with a lot of eyewitnesses, there will come a time when the eyewitness accounts will be evaluated alongside the physical evidence to make sure everything matches up. On that Saturday, an ambulance had arrived right away. Darren Wilson had been on an ambulance call just prior to the episode on Canfield, and the ambulance had been just minutes behind him. The EMTs determined that Brown was deceased. Since they were unable to do anything more until the crime scene team arrived, they left the scene.

The narrative that flew around via social media and the internet had it that we—I, specifically, as the face of the Ferguson police—had left the body in the street deliberately as a means of intimidating the local residents. Supposedly, I wanted to send a message that this could be anyone who hadn't behaved, that the Ferguson police were willing to gun people down in the middle of the street for no reason. At a symposium I attended at Harvard (which I discuss later), a professor essentially said as much, implying that I left the body in the street either as a deliberate gesture of disrespect, or simply because I didn't care. When the investigators were finally able to remove Michael Brown's body, they did so in the first available vehicle, a large black coroner's SUV. Again, the lack of ceremony was described online as an insult.

Had the body been moved before the scene had been thoroughly examined, that would have been grounds for claims of police misconduct. Damned if you do, damned if you don't. I chose to play it by the book and ensure a proper accounting for what happened that day. I wish there had been another option.

An issue that arose in those first few hours, and would become an ongoing focal point of the national conversation, had to do with the size of the police presence at the scene as well as tactics and equipment used. I'm a public servant, the chief of police in my city, sworn to safeguard the public. Protecting the people, homes, and businesses of Ferguson was what I was paid to do, and I was prepared to use whatever means available to maximize the safety of the public. Any of my counterparts from other agencies on the scene would say the same. I had ceded control of the investigation, but the scene on Canfield was still my responsibility, and I did not want it to get out of control. If officers are reporting a crowd that appears on the verge of rioting, the right and natural response is to bring in enough personnel to protect the innocent residents and the infrastructure of the neighborhood. The larger and more agitated the crowd became, the more officers were needed. Though their only purpose was to defend and protect, the influx of police, especially those in riot gear, was portrayed as a military invasion.

Again, I ask the reader to consider what the response might have been if the police presence on the scene had been insufficient. Did we not care enough about Canfield to send enough cops to protect it? Would we have been seen as permitting a riot to develop, content to let those residents trash the community in anger? Again, the police couldn't really win for losing; they had to take any and all steps, according to their training, to secure the public safety.

On that first Saturday, the public response had to do mostly with the large numbers of cops in protective gear, commonly described by people on social media as invading storm troopers, but the controversy would expand to cover tactics such as tear gas and the presence of large police vehicles that many would refer to as "military vehicles" and some would even—incorrectly—claim were tanks.

There was one police tactic that, in retrospect, may have been ill-advised, but even this reflected an understandable logic: the introduction of the dogs. I don't fault the county captain for calling in the canines. To his eyes, the crowd was becoming an angry mob. People shouted threats and grew physically aggressive. And yes, shots had rung out. The captain acted as he was trained, knowing that the dogs, trained in crowd control, could serve as a deterrent against violence while protecting the scene so the investigators could finish their work. Again, dogs are trained to be protective and defensive. They are not attack dogs, as some people portrayed them on social media. That captain didn't have the time to step back and consider the rapidly unfolding events in the context of history or public opinion.

Ironically, canines hadn't been used in a crowd situation in our area for as long as anyone could remember. I doubt if, in the heat of the moment, it would have occurred to any cop, myself included, how it would look for a predominantly white team of police officers to introduce dogs into a scene of overwhelmingly black onlookers. In all the public hand-wringing about the police response in Ferguson and elsewhere, people neglect to account for the mentality of trained police, who think first about serving the public. Bringing canines into the situation was not an attempt to silence protest. If anything, the dogs might have kept the protest from degenerating into a riot that would have drowned out real grievances. Nor was it a case of white authorities suppressing an angry black mob.

As night fell that Saturday, the intersection of Canfield and West Florissant began to feel like a street fair that had somehow gone terribly wrong. I had the feeling that as news spread about the shooting and the public protest, more and more people had the sense that something important and historic was happening in Ferguson, and they wanted to come and be a part of it. People were making their way to our town from farther and farther away, and the more time that passed, the more people showed up. The local officers on the scene all knew that they were no longer dealing with only Ferguson residents. It felt like we were patrolling some kind of twisted, hostile Woodstock festival.

All the years of experience and training could only take me so far in these uncharted waters. I think most of the other officers at the scene had the same sense of apprehension. That particular corner of Ferguson happens to fall in close proximity to a number of different jurisdictions, and while the total number of officers at the scene had been reduced, there was still a healthy police presence in the area, although none were actively engaged in crowd control.

A local radio station, 104.1, contacted me and asked for any comment or advice they could convey to their listeners. My response was to tell people the investigation needed to move forward and that would take time. After I signed off, the station told listeners that there would be no answers today. In contrast to the protesters at the scene demanding immediate answers and action, it provided a voice to calm fears and to avoid a rush for results now.

By midnight, people in the crowd began to find their way home, and as the numbers dwindled, the general tension in the air started to ebb a little. I remained in constant motion, walking around the area and talking to as many people as I could, explaining what was going on, what the police were trying to do, appealing for patience and calm. I finally went home around 2:30 am, after fourteen hours at the scene, thinking that maybe the fever had broken, that things would get back to normal soon. Even now, I find myself still surprised by how long the situation continued.

The next day, Sunday, the crowds had swelled again. I remember the sensation of being in a massive crowd that morning, but in retrospect, it still may only have been a couple hundred people, mostly centered around that main intersection of Canfield and West Florissant, but also now concentrating at other points, such as the Ferguson police station and the QuikTrip convenience store, a stone's throw from the shooting scene. Still believing that the episode was in the process of winding down, I turned my immediate attention to all the other problems and responsibilities that the shooting had triggered. First, I met John Shaw, the city manager, and other officials who needed reassurance that I had a handle on things at the street level. At the time, of course, I believed that I did. Next, I had to get to downtown St. Louis, where members of the press had started to gather. One of my assignments now was to speak to these reporters and provide as much information as possible.

That's where I was when I got a very anxious call from one of my commanders. He told me that the crowd had suddenly gotten "huge" and "threatening." Another Code 1000 had been called, and by the time I got back to Ferguson, it did indeed look like some kind of invasion was taking place.

Police cars were swarming the area, as were more specialized vehicles from the various tactical units that had arrived. Law enforcement began using these vehicles in the wake of the North Hollywood bank robbery shootout, which saw the police heavily outgunned, and the Columbine massacre. These were primarily large "people mover" vehicles, designed and built by LENCO in Pittsfield, Massachusetts, my hometown, ironically. Law enforcement use them to get large numbers of people quickly out of harm's way, and to safely insert hostage rescue teams, among other uses. They would later be described, often by people who clearly knew better, as "tanks." Many of the police officers now at the scene were wearing protective helmets and body armor, as well.

Indeed, the unrest in the crowd intensified throughout the day. By evening, random scuffles were breaking out across the area, and rocks were flying. Throngs of people blocked traffic, at one point even preventing an ambulance from getting through to someone in need of help. The tipping point for most of the police on hand came when the sound of gunfire filled the air. Nobody was shot, and we couldn't identify the source of the shots, but the presence of gunfire signaled that the situation was spiraling out of control.

There was a feeling of an impending attack that we would not be able to stop as we stood in solid lines of officers on three sides holding back thousands of people who seemed ready to attack. Behind us was a sea of police cars parked randomly down the street as far as we could see.

Standing there in the middle of West Florissant Avenue, it also began to feel like a reunion of sorts as many of my long-time friends and colleagues started to appear. Charles "Chuck" Thal was an undercover cop when I was a SWAT sergeant, and we had carried out many search warrants together. Now he was a bank president, business manager, entrepreneur, and volunteer police commander at a neighboring department. He was also director of the local police chiefs' association. Chuck called me daily to see what manpower I needed for the day's protests and riots. He was a fixture in the streets during the most violent times as well.

Others that showed up that night included most of the command staff of the St. Louis County Police Department, my alma mater. Captain Kurt Frisz and I flew helicopters together after I campaigned to bring him into the SWAT unit. He went on to become the most decorated officer in county PD history, twice winning the Medal of Valor, one of a very few to do so. Ken Cox, Ken Gregory, and Mike Dierkes, like Kurt, served with me in the SWAT unit. I had brought Kurt and Mike with me to the drug unit. County Chief Belmar had yet to arrive, which made Mike the ranking county officer on the scene.

As the crowd began to flow across jurisdictional boundaries, officers from every area department bravely arrived to assist, as they did for many weeks to come. Knowing the answer, I jokingly asked Mike, "So, who's in charge here?"

Without skipping a beat, he responded, "I'll flip you for it."

At about 9:00 a.m., someone set fire to the QuikTrip on West Florissant. Anybody who had spent any time at all in that neighborhood knew that the QuikTrip was one of its cornerstones. More than a simple convenience store, it was where many of the locals did their regular grocery shopping and got their morning coffee or cold drinks in summer. It was absolutely essential to many area residents who didn't own cars, a central meeting place, like the general store in an old prairie town. When I saw that place go up in flames, I knew in my heart that no one from Canfield or anywhere in Ferguson could have been responsible. It became clear to me in that moment that we were dealing with a problem that had outgrown our town. I texted my wife: "They're shooting at us and burned and looted QT. Who does that???" Outsiders—protesters, opportunists, agitators, maybe just thrill-seekers—had taken over, and even managed to shut down the city's website.

Within minutes of the QuikTrip catching fire, all hell broke loose. Tear gas was deployed to disperse the crowd, but the mob was a long way from calling it a night. Groups of people went off in every direction. Looting, vandalism, and fighting spread in all directions, covering an area within perhaps a two-mile radius, with the intersection at its center. Gunfire filled the air.

By then, Chief Belmar had arrived on the scene. After taking stock of the situation, he and I jumped into my black Tahoe and drove around the area, trying to assess both the existing damage and the looming threat. Word came quickly of trouble at the huge Walmart store several blocks away. Shots had been fired, and an unknown number of people were trapped inside the store. Jon and I drove up to see dozens of rioters looting the nearby strip mall. After the Walmart had been secured and the employees freed, Jon and I walked back toward my vehicle just in time to see an old yellow pickup truck peeling out of the parking lot. An arm reached out of the truck window and more shots were fired. We gave chase, but quickly lost the truck in the chaos that had suddenly consumed Ferguson. One officer was at another shopping center where five cars full of looters pulled up in plain sight of him and smashed store windows, stealing whatever they could grab. The looting went on for hours and although we had made dozens of arrests by the time things settled down around 3:00 a.m., I felt that this was only the beginning. Sadly, I was right.

Everything changed that Sunday night. The burning of the QuikTrip stands out in my mind as a pivotal moment. I understood then that the situation in Ferguson had become bigger than all of us.

When I got the job as police chief in Ferguson, it truly felt like coming home. I had lived and worked in the area for close to fifty years, having moved there from Massachusetts as a boy.

I had taken an EMT class at night while I was studying musical theater in college. I found I loved the work, and moved on to get my paramedic license and took a job with a hospital-based ambulance service in St. Louis County.

Working alongside police officers every day inspired me to follow what I can only describe as a calling to join their ranks. I very quickly grew anxious to move beyond patrolling a beat. I served as an undercover narcotics officer, burglary detective, SWAT team leader, and helicopter instructor pilot, and eventually rose to the rank of captain. Through my work on major task forces, I built relationships throughout various local, state, and even federal law enforcement agencies, as well as with politicians in St. Louis County and the state government of Missouri. More importantly, I believed I had become a part of a large community, with connections to business and development figures, religious organizations, and community leaders and organizers from various groups. Together, we were making more of a difference than I had ever thought possible.

In many respects, Ferguson in 2014 wasn't much different from the town I knew as a kid, except for the changing demographics. Like many inner suburbs around big cities, it had seen the rapid growth of the black middle class, as many white families moved out to newer suburbs farther out. And, for a while, the town's economy had become less stable. Although Emerson Electric remained, the area had lost a lot of jobs over the years.

What very few people understand, however, is that by the time I came on board as chief of police, Ferguson was on the move, looked upon by many as a "renaissance community." The downtown area was redeveloped and bustling with new shops and restaurants, including a popular microbrewery and pub, giving residents a reason to stay in town for their nightlife, which meant spending their dollars at home. It would be no exaggeration to say that Ferguson had become a destination town for shopping and entertainment. Much of the downtown commercial growth came thanks to the support of a local business owner, Joe Lonero, who, along with his family, chose not to bail on his hometown, as so many successful people do, but to remain in Ferguson and to invest in the future of the town, psychologically as well as financially.

At the same time, a team of community leaders, led by City Manager John Shaw and Mayor James Knowles III, worked hard to attract other new businesses to Ferguson. A new shopping center opened, along with several big-box national chain stores, creating hundreds of new jobs and bringing new tax revenue into the town. The sense that people in Ferguson cared deeply about working together to build a stronger community deepened my own commitment and confirmed that I had chosen well to come back to town to work.

I enjoyed being a part of the town's resurgence. My relationships in town crossed racial and socioeconomic lines. Black leaders in the city routinely invited me to events across the community, from the simple pleasure of singing the national anthem at local events to running public education programs and organizing community pressure on deadbeat absentee landlords. People all over town knew me and sought me out. It's so sad that Ferguson is now fixed in the minds of the American public as a symbol of inequality and conflict, when it seemed we were doing so much that was positive. In fact, just prior to that crazy summer, the city council was in discussion about annexing and incorporating one of the neighboring areas. It was this proposal that triggered the "Ferguson Annexation Survey Report" by a University of Missouri–St. Louis professor that addressed not only public satisfaction, but many of the municipal plans and policies that would come under such intense fire later. The extremely positive findings of that study—findings that the Department of Justice chose to ignore—further convinced me that we were on the right track in Ferguson.

The point is not that things were all rosy in our town. Far from it. As I'll discuss throughout this book, we had our share of systemic ills in schools and housing, and many other factors contributed to trap some residents in a seemingly inescapable cycle of poverty. But I had believed, deep down, that the people of Ferguson were working together and moving the town in the right direction.

When I finally made it home on Sunday, I was as confused as I was exhausted. Had we misunderstood the mood of the town? Had we underestimated the anger simmering just under the surface? Was the outrage we had just witnessed on the street homegrown, or somehow ignited by outside forces? The only thing I knew for sure was that in the course of a single day, Ferguson had become almost unrecognizable to me.

Chapter Two

The Media Feeding Frenzy

An acquaintance who works in network news once said he couldn't imagine anything more hellish than being at the center of a major media frenzy. He talked about how the media chew people up for a few weeks, turning all the major players in a real-life event into cartoon characters, then moves on to the next story, leaving people's lives in tatters. He said he wouldn't wish it on his worst enemy—and this is from someone actually in the industry. More amazingly, this was also before the advent of smart phones, social media, and crowdsourced online journalism, all of which have made the problem so much worse.

Don't get me wrong. I'm not a dinosaur longing for the days of three TV channels and rotary telephones. I'm as excited as the next guy about new technologies and devices, and happy to make use of them all. We have gained so much through the constant access to information, the new windows into other people's lives and cultures offered by social media, and the greater reach of the news media. Having a handful of corporations controlling what we watched and what we read was never a great thing, but we've gotten into a situation now where there are no controls, no filters, no checks and balances. In fact, we're bombarded with images and information all day long, and what I've learned is that it's harder than ever to find out where a story or "fact" comes from, to figure out what's genuinely credible.

My colleagues and I had a lot to contend with in Ferguson during the summer of 2014, but the thing we were least prepared to deal with was the tidal wave of misinformation that washed across the country. It started within moments of Michael Brown's death and ultimately triggered responses in people that endangered more lives, in law enforcement and the general public. It's a safe bet that even before I first heard about it, news of the shooting had already spread.

As I've said, the incident took place in a populous housing project near a busy crossroads, where neighbors would have heard or seen something. They phoned and texted neighbors, posted and tweeted on the internet, so that a crowd of people had already started to gather before I arrived. Suspicion, and in some cases even outright hostility, was palpable. What that meant to me was that someone had already communicated the idea that something bad had gone down, something unjust.

Remember that the first call I received after arriving at the scene that Saturday was from John Shaw, the Ferguson city manager, alerting me to the fact that a story was already out, the public was hearing about it, and already the city and the police were being painted in a bad light. Shaw wanted me to manage or control that, or maybe even get out in front of it, as they say, but the shooting had only just taken place, and investigators were at that moment trying to gather facts and evidence. I hadn't even seen anybody from the news media there by the time I got that call, but a little later, when a news crew from a local St. Louis television station interviewed me, seeking details of the shooting for their story, I explained the situation again. *The shooting had only just taken place.* It's easy to understand that people want information, but there was nothing I could have said that would have helped either Michael Brown or Darren Wilson. Quite the opposite, in fact, since I barely knew anything myself. I didn't want anything I said tainting the investigation, creating unfounded preconceptions about either Brown or Wilson, or inflaming the public.

I didn't realize the horse was well out of the barn. People were already talking about the shooting at Canfield, so when an interview was broadcast live, anybody who wanted to see me or the city management as dodging questions or covering something up already had something they could hang their hat on.

What I didn't know was that at roughly the same time, Dorian Johnson was giving his own live interview. Johnson, a friend of Michael Brown, had been with him at the time of the encounter with Darren Wilson. Johnson told a terrifying story about how he and his friend were innocently walking down the street when a cop came and started harassing and threatening them, and in the ensuing altercation, Michael Brown put his hands in the air in peaceful surrender, at which point Officer Wilson shot him dead.

"Hands up, don't shoot." It came directly from Dorian Johnson's uncorroborated, unfiltered account, delivered live on television. It became the single, simplistic defining expression about the incident. It also became the default assumption behind all the early media coverage. Everybody wanted to know what went wrong, how something like this could happen. "Hands up, don't shoot" became the assumed fact that would have to be disproven, rather than something that should have needed proof from the start.

I didn't see Johnson's interview until much later, when I got home on Saturday. I recall being dumbfounded and thinking, "That can't be right." And we did indeed find later that only moments before that encounter, Johnson had been captured on security video with Brown, while Brown committed a strong-arm robbery of a convenience store. Months later the hands up narrative, as well as Johnson's description of the initial encounter between Brown and Officer Wilson, were shown to be false by the FBI and the Department of Justice.

But as I watched the news that night, I knew nothing about Dorian Johnson and had no opinion of his credibility as a person. I only knew his story didn't make any sense. A cop would not reach up from behind the wheel of a car with one arm to assault a man. A cop wouldn't threaten to shoot from inside the car. Why would he fire multiple rounds into that man for no reason, a man who had his hands up in surrender? Every instinct I had told me Dorian Johnson's story was wrong.

But I knew my officers, and the people buying this account did not. They had a one-word answer to the question of why Darren Wilson would've shot Michael Brown: racism. Once the idea was planted that Wilson was a racist shooting a man, secure he could get away with it because he was a cop and the other man was "only a black man," it overwhelmed the illogic of the rest of it.

Perhaps the hardest lesson I've had to process since that day is that for some in minority populations, Johnson's version of events had the ring of absolute truth. Just like my reflex, based on history and personal experience, was to think, "No way," the reflex of many African Americans was, "Of course. Same as always." If I had not known my officers, if I had suspected them of what the crowd suspected, hell, I'd have been out there protesting, too.

So when Dorian Johnson stepped in front of the cameras, to all appearances without motive to tell anything but the truth, the media had ready-made good guys and bad guys—the innocent and oppressed young black men, and the arrogant and unfeeling racist police officers.

It's important to step back and recognize how advantageous this is to media companies that need to make the most of their news cycles. A story about police brutality could have legs, especially once it generated ongoing protests. Reporters and camera crews had access to what seemed like an unlimited number of witnesses and onlookers willing to talk to them, just as they knew I was always available to them wherever I happened to be, on the street, at the police station, or at city hall.

I can't say for sure if, at the height of the media frenzy, protesters and activists got more airtime than police sources or city officials, but I know that we absolutely were treated differently. After a lifetime as a public servant, I was suddenly chief of the bad guys. Community relations were not perfect in Ferguson, but after years of focused, city-wide initiatives, we had made great strides forward and were in constant dialogue with neighborhood associations and community groups. Yet, when a reporter frames you in their camera shot with a hostile crowd in the background and asks how you and other officials could be so naive and unaware of public resentment, there is no correct response. It's truly like asking someone, "When did you stop beating your wife?"

Representatives of Ferguson eventually just started nodding as if in acknowledgement, just to put a quick end to the misguided questions. We all understood that concentrated poverty makes public housing complexes hot spots of violent crime. Was there a disproportionate police presence in the Canfield projects? Possibly, yes, but we were also there as educators and organizers. Plenty of our officers took on secondary employment in these neighborhoods, hoping to provide information, education, and resources to the residents.

Why didn't the reporters ever ask citizens, "What convinced you the shooting couldn't be justified? What made you presume the police would cover that up? Do you know the officer? How do you know what really happened?"

I wanted to know what really happened. In every interview I gave—and I couldn't wait for my next chance to make the point—I reiterated that I wanted exactly what the protesters wanted: justice. I wanted to know what had actually happened, to reach the correct conclusion, so that we could take positive action based on that knowledge.

But members of the media, whom I had perhaps naively expected to be advocates for impartial justice, approached me with the assumption that I was hiding something or had an agenda of protecting the officer and department, no matter what.

Before I go further, I want to say that oversimplification in a political conversation is a common problem. We lump together huge groups of seemingly similar people to discuss them as if everyone who falls in the same group feels and acts the same way; that's what people have done with police, and what they have done with poor people, and with the African American population and so many other groups. I don't want to fall into the same trap when talking about the media. They are not a monolithic block.

The age of the big three networks is over. There are dozens of news outlets competing for ratings, and ratings are revenue. Conflict draws greater audiences than headlines about calm returning to Ferguson.

The bigger the audience reached by a particular outlet, the less nuanced and more sensational their coverage of Ferguson was. It is dangerous for journalists to have a horse in the race that they're covering.

We can start with the twenty-four-hour television news channels, such as CNN. There were individual correspondents and interviewers who asked intelligent questions, but those efforts happened within the context of the overall presentation of the story, which sought to maintain the level of explosive drama that would keep drawing as many viewers as possible.

As has happened with so many big news stories in the past, news channels created eye-catching graphics about the conflict, always accompanied by dark and ominous musical themes, to open each news hour or new program. I'm not saying that the drama didn't exist, but I am confident the conflict they were both promoting and reporting grew because of that coverage. It has long been known that people behave differently when the cameras show up. By the time the rioting in Ferguson reached its most dangerous levels, it was clear to all of us who lived there that the main agitators were from somewhere else; they had come to Ferguson to be a part of what they had been watching on television.

Even the twenty-four-hour news networks differed in their coverage, largely due to the prevailing political agendas of each one. People like to describe CNN as the more liberal network and FOX as the more right-leaning, and that's generally how they behaved in Ferguson. CNN's Don Lemon was never less than gracious and polite, but he smilingly asked me a string of loaded questions designed to get me to say something inadvertently damaging about Michael Brown, his family, or his community, or about the investigation or the policing of Ferguson. These were no-win interviews for me; even if I succeeding in dodging the bullets he fired at me, I ended up looking shifty and evasive.

Lemon stated on camera that the "most disturbing aspect" about the situation in Ferguson was that I was unaware of the animosity of the African American population toward the police. He said this, however, without giving any context. He never mentioned the commitment I had demonstrated to improving community relations, nor the successes we had achieved in that area. He didn't talk about the time I and my officers spent establishing programs within the public housing projects, tracking down absentee landlords, building community organizations, or just being present in the neighborhood, getting to know people. None of that ever came out because Lemon, like so many other reporters, neither knew about that nor cared enough to ask about it. It seemed like this man believed that either his position or his race gave him the license to pass judgment on a situation about which he knew almost nothing.

Jake Tapper, another CNN correspondent, filed more egregious reports from the streets of Ferguson, describing scenes that were practically the opposite of what was being captured on camera in the background. I remember him at one point going on about the "peaceful protesters" while fires raged behind him and a protester could clearly be seen throwing a smoke bomb at police. Their running theme of peaceful protesters and aggressive policing persisted, despite the nonstop rocks, bottles, urine, and death threats faced by police. As far as Tapper and most other news people were concerned, if there were no active looting or arson immediately visible, the protests were peaceful.

Tapper brought things to a head about ten days after the shooting in a memorable report that won him a lot of praise. In the report, he seemed to drop any pretense of responsible journalism and just went off, extemporaneously and subjectively. It was passionate and indelible, and in my opinion, completely misguided. Tapper managed to douse this fire with gasoline.

He had the camera pan down the street to show the protesters "way down there," well in the distance, milling about doing nothing much. Then he directed the viewers' attention in the other direction, to the police "dressed for combat," in his words. Tapper itemized the semiautomatic weapons, shields, helmets, and so on, and expressed outrage that this was happening "in America." "Why they're doing this, I don't know. There's no reason for this . . . There's no threat here that merits this . . . This doesn't make any sense." He went on and on.

Jake Tapper "didn't know," but all he had to do was what any serious journalist should have done. He could have *asked*, but he didn't. This was ten days into the rioting, ten days of relentless attacks on property and on police, ten days of death threats issued via social media and directly to our faces. Ten days of "the only good cop is a dead cop!" Also, it was ten days in which no one had been injured. I'll discuss these tactics and equipment in a later chapter on policing, but suffice it to say that Tapper's big moment on camera might have made for compelling television, but it was beyond bad journalism. His reporting was utterly irresponsible.

FOX had its own very different view of the situation: to lay all the blame for the crisis at the feet of President Obama and his administration. This proved to be a double-edged sword for me. I had to stay incredibly focused in interviews, so as to avoid inadvertently adding my voice to the network's long-standing opposition to the policies of the administration. At the same time, however, I believed FOX was absolutely right in calling out the administration and the Department of Justice for their premature and biased comments. On Monday, August 11, for instance, President Obama made a statement to the nation. He rightly spoke about the need to step back, to de-escalate violence, to determine what actually happened and to see that justice would be done. But then he undid all that good sense by stating:

> The local authorities—including the police—have a responsibility to be open and transparent about how they are investigating that death, and how they are protecting the people in their communities. . . . There's also no excuse for police to use excessive force against peaceful protests, or to throw protesters in jail for lawfully exercising their First Amendment rights. And here, in the United States of America, police should not be bullying or arresting journalists who are just trying to do their jobs and report to the American people on what they see on the ground.

Here was the president, confirming, by implication, the nation's collective misunderstanding: peaceful protestors, lying and bullying cops unlawfully throwing people in jail and denying them basic rights. I understand the president's desire to help restore calm, but how the hell were we supposed to do our jobs after that?

None of this was about national politics for me. I had no predisposition against the Obama administration prior to the trouble in Ferguson, and even as infuriated as I felt, I did not want to frame the situation in terms of party politics. I appeared more than once on FOX, most notably on Sean Hannity's show, where he spoke very supportively about law enforcement. I remember him reading a statement from the leader of a national police organization that was critical of President Obama while reinforcing some sensible points that I supported. I knew that if I said I agreed with the statement, it would have amped up the hostility against the police in Ferguson even more. I didn't comment on the statement, except to say that I was "just a policeman" who didn't want to get involved in anybody's political agenda. I have no doubt that efforts like this to stay out of the fray only reinforced the public perception that I was one more public official afraid to speak frankly about anything. Still, a bunch of articles suddenly appeared with headlines screaming, "Chief Jackson turns to Hannity to get his message across." The simple fact that I was on FOX News at all became fodder for the conspiracy theorists.

Where FOX got it right was in their condemnation of Obama's representative, Attorney General Eric Holder. Holder arrived in Ferguson about a week and a half after the shooting. Here was the country's top law enforcement official making a huge show of coming to this center of unrest, but his display had nothing to do with supporting law enforcement. I heard he visited the police command post on West Florissant Avenue, but I never met or even saw the man. He never sought me out, nor did he ever meet with any Ferguson city officials. Instead, he visited Michael Brown's mother, as well as Ron Johnson, the African American Missouri highway patrol captain assigned to Ferguson, and then Holder stated publicly his goal of seeking "justice for Michael Brown." Justice isn't for one person or one group more than for everyone. Justice is equal and impartial, either for everybody or for nobody. No one should know that better than the US attorney general.

It was actually in an interview with Jason Carroll on CNN that I lost my temper a little bit about Holder. Less than two months after the shooting, Holder was already calling for "wholesale change" in the Ferguson police department, and I made it clear that I considered that way out of line. Holder's tacit confirmation that this had been a bad shooting, broadcast live, not only cemented the Justice Department's biased stance in the upcoming investigation but also turned up the heat of public anger and raised the level of the violence and rioting in Ferguson. He made the job of law enforcement even harder than it already was, putting the public and police both at greater risk. At one point, I even felt the need to move my family away from the threat. This was the true nature of the "support" that local law enforcement received from the top federal law enforcement official, but I'll return to the subject of the Department of Justice, and its own rush to judgment, later in the book.

In the end, both major news channels got a few things right and quite a lot wrong, despite their different political bents. Interestingly, the network with the most objective and even-handed coverage, in my view, was the now defunct Al Jazeera America (formerly Al Gore's Current TV network). Maybe that shows how dangerous it is for journalists to have a horse in the race they're covering.

What we see is as important as what we hear and what we read, and most of us often forget to ask what it is we're *not* seeing. If a television crew repeatedly points its camera at a line of police officers in riot gear, or captures the arrival of armored police rescue vehicles from an angle that makes them look bigger and more imposing that they might actually be, those images are instantly seared in viewers' minds. If the same station only shows, for comparison, protesters quietly singing and holding flickering candles, that impression likewise lingers. That's pretty much what happened every day in Ferguson. There wasn't a whole lot of footage of cops helping people to safety, or meeting with community leaders, or in conversation with residents and protesters. There wasn't much footage of rioting crowds screaming, "Fuck the police!" and "Death to cops!" or flipping over random vehicles or hurling bottles of frozen water or urine at police officers. But there seemed to be no end of footage of people—usually people from someplace other than Ferguson—weeping in public, or unleashing some vicious tirade about bad policing.

Newspapers joined into this twisting of reality, too. I distinctly remember one incident during the height of the protests: A clergyman—not someone anybody recognized as local—was heading up a mob of angry protesters, who also called themselves clergymen, as it moved toward a line of police. He was urging the protesters to confront the officers verbally with obscenities and threats, and the moment grew very tense. A still photographer captured an image of this face-off, and when it ran in the newspaper, it carried a caption that read "members of the clergy minister to police." I complained loudly to the newspaper staff and received a message from a top official saying they inadvertently used the word "minister" instead of "confront." The next day there was a photo showing an officer speaking to a rabbi with the previous day's "ministering" comment. I considered it a message from the paper letting me know they buy ink by the barrel.

Generally, though, newspapers tended to bring more subtlety and nuance to the story. Local media are often criticized for sensationalizing the news, but I found overall that secondary media outlets, particularly those based near Ferguson, had more balanced and detailed coverage. Maybe that was because they weren't in the same mad race for ratings as the national media, or because they weren't using Ferguson's pain to promote their on-camera stars or their political agendas. I think that in the case of the local newspapers and television stations, the fairness was connected to their deep knowledge of the people and the environment. These people had been covering Ferguson and the surrounding towns for a very long time. They knew me, and understood my standing in the town and the work our police force was trying to do in town. It was only natural that local journalists would be the first, if not the only ones to think, "Wait, that can't be right" regarding the "hands up, don't shoot" narrative or the depiction of the Ferguson police as a bunch of corrupt and racist storm troopers. I'm grateful to some of those reporters, especially a few at the *St. Louis Post-Dispatch* and radio 97.1, who tried to balance the record with positive profiles and who provided a forum in which I could try to get our story across. I don't believe that was a function of favoritism, but more of simple common sense.

The leadership in Ferguson did make one attempt to take control of the media narrative, an effort that completely backfired and in the end surely hurt more than it helped. Recognizing that we were in way over our heads in this crisis, we brought in public relations professionals who specialized in "crisis management." The first PR consultants were two smart young women who were going to improve our messaging. Almost immediately, they started receiving threats at their offices, and quit within a couple weeks. The city replaced them with an African American man who was just as well-intentioned but just as overwhelmed by the pace and the intensity of the situation.

Up until that point, I had spoken off-the-cuff with the press, not just making myself available to them but seeking them out, trying to establish myself as an open and available source of information. Unfortunately, the only time I let my interaction with press be managed by PR people (the first of the two PR consultants) was for what might have been our most critical press conference. It was the first time I was scripted for an event, and it would be the last time.

The investigation had a number of moving parts, and while we were all committed to transparency, the release of certain pieces of information required delicacy. First, we had not yet released Darren Wilson's name to the public, partly for his safety, and partly because the investigators were still gathering information and evidence. We were under a lot of pressure from the DOJ, the Missouri state government, the press, and activists to release the name of the officer who shot Michael Brown. Reporters and the public were clamoring for the name, and beginning to suggest other officer's names, thus putting them in danger. During my press conferences, reporters would ask why I wouldn't release Darren Wilson's name. I was convinced no good could come from releasing his name, which certainly turned out to be the case, but they started asking specific names of cops on the department, as in "Was it Officer White?" The first few times they did that I said no, to keep those officers from being targeted since Darren was out of the area. As each officer's name was put forward, he would be ID'd in social media and sought out by the violent groups pouring into Ferguson. I soon realized that they were going to ask every officer's name until they got the right one. My mistake was in making a specific denial instead of saying that I could neither confirm nor deny. If, when they finally got to Darren's name, I had been saying, "I can neither confirm nor deny that," it would not have been obvious that it was the right name.

At the same time, the investigators had in their possession the security video from Ferguson Market & Liquor, a convenience store, which appeared to show Michael Brown roughing up the shopkeeper and grabbing a pack of cigarillos. Not being part of the actual investigative team, I hadn't even seen the video, and I didn't know how it was relevant to the shooting, if at all. The city and the police department were getting bombarded with Freedom of Information Act (FOIA) requests. One reporter who had found out about the video stood in my office demanding to see it, even scribbling out a FOIA request on the spot, on a scrap of paper. At the time, I didn't stop to ask how any reporters even knew there was a video to ask about. Later, the conspiracy theorists suggested that someone on the police had leaked the existence of the store video, so that the press would ask about it, giving the police an excuse to release it, which they would not otherwise have had. I have to believe that there probably was an internal leak somewhere, and that it was not planned or calculated as part of some larger plot, but resulted from frustration at the false narrative.

Everybody understood that releasing the video might trigger a protest. I honestly believed that what people wanted was a full and detailed understanding, and that at the very least, the video would offer an alternative to the portrayal of Brown as a "gentle giant." Since it seemed we had to release both pieces of information at the same time, I thought it might soften the impact of making Darren Wilson's name public.

Those involved did everything we could to smooth the way for this release of information. We set up a meeting with Michael Brown's mother to inform her. Although she wasn't present, she had a representative there. We were able to tell representatives of the NAACP and ACLU, and the Department of Justice Community Relations Service, who later claimed they asked for the video NOT to be released, although no record of any such claim exists. We cleared it with Chief Jon Belmar, who was leading the local investigation, the FBI, and prosecuting attorney Bob McCulloch. We even informed the shopkeeper. We let Darren know to be prepared. Soon after, local news Channel 5 flew their helicopter over Darren's house and broadcast images of it on the news. That reckless move enraged everyone, not just the police. Apparently realizing they had crossed the line, the news director called me to apologize for what he called a terrible decision. I believed he was sincere, but the damage had been done—to Darren, his neighbors, and to Channel 5's relationship with the police.

On the morning of the press conference where we would release a large packet containing both these items, I was handed a script. The script itself made me feel nervous and unnatural, and the television cameras captured my discomfort. It didn't help that I was forced to wear glasses to read the thing and had to keep taking them on and off. I looked stiff, and sounded formal and stilted, not at all like myself, reading instead of talking, fumbling with my glasses rather than looking people in the eye. When I watched the video later, I thought, "That's a guy who's not on the level," which is exactly how some of the press reported it.

We distributed the packet of information and I suggested everyone familiarize themselves with it, and prepare any questions for a second press conference that afternoon. I was given some talking points for that afternoon session, but thankfully, no script. Still, I wasn't prepared for the grilling that was to come. Almost immediately, reporters asked very pointedly why we had released the video at that time. They suggested that we acted to tarnish Michael Brown's reputation while deflecting attention away from Darren Wilson, whom everybody just assumed by now to be a cold-blooded killer of young black men.

I answered with the truth: that I released the video at that time "because you asked for it." I had a desk full of FOIA requests relating to all types of information in the packet and had to comply. The press now had everything that I could lawfully release and they seemed upset about it. I would not have chosen to make that information public, in that way, at that time.

I even caught flak from within the law enforcement community. The day before that press conference was the day I learned, unofficially from the media, that Missouri governor Jay Nixon had assigned Ron Johnson, a captain from the highway patrol, to take over security at Canfield and West Florissant, the center of the protests. That led to the fairy-tale "Night of Peace," for which Ron Johnson took credit. While people were digesting the video release, talk radio was abuzz with listener comments like "The video is doctored," "Those aren't the clothes Michael Brown was wearing that day," and "This is a page right out of the Police Character Assassination Playbook, whenever a white cop kills a black man." The violence that followed was blamed on me, for deliberately undoing all of the good will created by Ron Johnson. Never mind that there was no Night of Peace. The narrative now became: "Not even Ron Johnson can stop this new rage!" By the time I formally met Johnson, he was already bitter, believing it was wrong of me not to inform him in advance about the video. That was totally illogical, but nonetheless, it soured our relationship before it even got started.

I don't think it's a surprise to anybody that the big news media follow the rules of the entertainment industry as much as the rules of traditional journalism. It's something that I'm sure I knew, but I never really thought consciously about because it never affected me or my world so directly. I should have been prepared, but I'll say in all honesty, what I was not prepared for was the uncontrollable impact of social media. That was the real wild animal in the room, and nobody knew how to deal with it. When it comes to social media, there simply are no rules. Digital and wireless technologies, the internet—all of it has revolutionized society, and mostly for the better. It's brought the whole world closer together, but at the same time has created a kind of wild west of instantaneous communications. In the short time since the crisis in Ferguson, how many cell phone videos involving interactions between police and the public have gone viral? On the one hand, I'm as interested as any other citizen in what these videos reveal, and how we can use them to bring about positive social change. On the other hand, I know from experience how dangerous it can be to form conclusions based on incomplete evidence and hearsay, and the fiery online cries of injustice.

When John Shaw, the city manager, reached me on my cell phone shortly after I arrived at the scene on that first

Saturday, the internet had already starting blowing up with news about Ferguson. At first, it was neighborhood residents texting their friends or making posts about the shooting on Twitter, Facebook, and Instagram. Naturally, those posts and tweets were first seen by friends in the general vicinity, which generated the early crowds. Soon enough, though, they were reaching ever-widening circles of friends and other social networks. Admittedly, we had been blind to all this internet activity, but by the second day, we were all painfully aware of how far behind we were in the social media conversation.

It seemed a pretty straightforward matter to handle the traditional media, because you could have access to the same audiences. If a television station ran a story, you could call a press conference and present information to counter it or to enhance it. You could seek out camera crews and reporters on the ground and speak directly to those audiences, and that was something I did every chance I could. And, I looked forward to every press conference as an opportunity to speak directly to the public and, I hoped, restore some order and sanity to the situation. I'm still forced to shake my head and wonder how I came to be a symbol of evasiveness and official covering up, when I spent so much time seeking out and speaking to the news media.

What it took us a while to really understand is you had to respond to any media activity through that same media. The only way to keep pace with social media was to have an active presence and following in those internet spaces, and we just didn't have that. Even after we wised up about social media, the best we could really hope for was to monitor it and learn how and where protesters were planning gatherings or other actions. The FBI was keeping a finger on that pulse, and let me know that hackers were targeting me specifically, as well as other officers that they identified through social media sites. We believed there was no way any account attached to the Ferguson police or city leadership was going to attract a meaningful following.

The thing about social media is that nothing gets filtered. Even in the least reputable news outlets, there are editors or producers or somebody making decisions about what gets run and what doesn't. They may not spend as much time as they should fact-checking or verifying, but at least somebody is making some kind of value judgment on the content. No such bars are set on Facebook or on Twitter. The only way to measure the value of an idea or an argument is to count the number of people who have seen or reacted to the post. How many "likes"? How many "retweets"? These are fundamentally meaningless statistics, but at the same time, they are hugely meaningful. The more people who engage with an idea, no matter how crackpot or unproven it might be, the more that idea becomes part of the accepted narrative and the conversation.

The issue becomes even more confusing because nowadays, big-name reporters for national publications and television broadcasts also have individual Twitter accounts, where they post observations and side commentary that may not make it onto the air or into their articles. Does anybody think that those celebrity correspondents apply the same journalistic standards to their Twitter feeds that they do in their regular jobs? Does anybody think their followers are conscious of the distinction? Those distinctions grew blurry with time. We know that in the first hours and days, crowds were drawn to Ferguson through social media traffic, but soon, the coverage of the unrest by traditional media became the magnet. And, I have no doubt that the continued focus and coverage kept the conflict boiling long after there were any points left to be made by any protests.

Meanwhile, there's a kind of Darwinian aspect to social media. Everybody has something to say, but only some people rise above the noise and develop big followings. These "livestreamers," for lack of a better term, basically controlled the protest, directing traffic, organizing and announcing assemblies, and setting the mood. They sent out streaming video in real time, across social media, projecting their own propaganda and opinions. Some were already public figures, including politicians like Maria Chappelle-Nadal, a Missouri state senator who took on a leadership role in the protests, largely through social media. One night, she sent out a tweet directing protesters to the police station, then called me up to say I should just "give them the street." I told her that wasn't going to happen, and asked why she wasn't looking after her constituency, who needed to use that street. (In fact, the senator neglected to tell me that she had been the source of the tweet. I only learned that later, from a reporter.) Chappelle-Nadal and I had worked together before and were on friendly terms, but the argument that ensued that night put an end to that. The next day, she denied posting the initial tweet and called me a "boldfaced liar" on television.

These streamers constantly broadcast live cell phone video from the protests, often deliberately putting officers' lives at risk by zooming in on their ID badges so that the public could have their names and track them down, which they were able to do by hacking or "doxing" personal information from their Facebook accounts. When protesters in fact started showing up at some officers' homes, we had officers remove their name tags, and then, incredibly, caught a ton of flak from the Justice Department, who insisted it was illegal to have officers go out in public without that identification.

The streamers could draw huge crowds by announcing they'd be filming and streaming at a particular location.

In a bizarre twist, there was one incident when a couple of CNN reporters showed up at one of those assemblies and got chased out because they weren't "real journalists." All the crowd wanted was to be part of the new online media.

In the two years since Michael Brown's death in Ferguson, a number of stories about black men dying at the hands of white police officers have received widespread media attention. Some of these incidents have been recorded on cell phones and then shared with the public via the internet. At least one of these tragedies, in Minnesota, was partially streamed live as it was happening. As smartphones proliferate in this country, virtually everyone is walking around with a camera and a microphone in their pocket or their handbag. The same device that can capture important words and images can also transmit them instantaneously around the world. And things will undoubtedly get much more complicated—and not necessarily any clearer—as more and more police begin wearing body cameras on the job. That is sure to open up all kinds of new areas of criminal law and civil rights laws for police and the public to negotiate.

Without question, incidents involving police use of deadly force must be thoroughly investigated. Even the most die-hard supporters of law enforcement have had to grapple with the police behavior that turns up on some videos. But not every case has a simple explanation, and not every case fits into the same black-and-white, good guy/bad guy model that the media like to promote. It's up to all of us to ask the hard questions and avoid the easy answers, to examine the sources of all news accounts, to separate reality from the oversimplification of media sound bites and ratings-driven hype of commercial news/entertainment outlets.

A great deal has changed in America since the summer of 2014. The media themselves have become a trigger point for the deepening polarization of the country. To a lot of people, the media have become a great big joke, the people who got it all wrong in November of 2016 and don't speak for the real America. An equal number hold out hope that the media will act as a voice of reason in unpredictable times. Now, instead of both sides complaining about biased media outlets manipulating and selectively assembling facts, we're all talking about "fake news." It seems like all of a sudden, much of the news we read and see is about which other news stories are real and which aren't.

Watching the events in Ferguson from the inside, I saw with my own eyes how "fake news" springs out of almost nowhere, and how quickly it takes over everybody's consciousness. As often as not, there wasn't any deliberate attempt to deceive, and the false narrative didn't start out as a partisan message. It could just be an unfiltered statement or random observation that caught somebody's attention online and then suddenly made its way around the internet and around the world at the speed of light. This is what happened with Dorian Johnson's statement about Michael Brown attempting to surrender with his hands up at the moment he was shot. It didn't matter whether the statement was true or not. It didn't even matter whether Johnson believed it or not when he said it. All that matters is that it went viral, and so did the narrative that went with it, pieced together with other random bits of information that were floating around.

As we saw, the same thing could happen with images. I can't count the number of times I know that news cameras took pictures of protesters keeping calm and behaving themselves appropriately, while a block away, out of the frame, other protesters were throwing rocks and bottles and bags of urine at police or turning over cars. Just as often, the exact opposite happened. News stations broadcast clashes between rioters and police that were taking place just around the corner from a much larger peaceful protest. Although these images also were picked up and reposted hundreds, even thousands, of times, they probably weren't as random. News channels had to have made editorial decisions about what they would shoot—usually what was the easiest to get and most dramatic—and also about what they would broadcast.

My wife, who was often as close to the action as I was, still finds it all totally surreal. One of the ways she stayed involved in the Ferguson community was to deliver Meals on Wheels to sick and elderly residents. On many days, her deliveries took her within a block of some of the most menacing and violent protests. But even that close, the life of the town kept on keeping on. The people to whom she brought meals were calm and comfortable inside their homes, watching on television the events unfolding just a block away. For them, it might as well have been across town or across the country. In fact, several times, as she left the houses, the owners would tell her not to bother locking the door behind her. Even as the media were showing riots and upheaval just outside, these residents felt secure in the Ferguson they knew, and told my wife that they didn't recognize the town they were seeing on the news.

Maybe we can all learn a valuable lesson from these events, starting with the Ferguson riots and culminating with the most recent presidential election. We've all been joking for years that "you can't believe what you read on the internet," but the time has come to acknowledge that it isn't really a joke. Whether it's something we read on our Facebook or Twitter feed, or a story reported by a name-brand national news outlet with a history of journalistic integrity, we, as citizens, are responsible for assessing each new piece of news on our own. Who made it public, and do they have an agenda? Where did they get their facts, and do we believe they are actually facts? Did anybody fact-check or corroborate? And most importantly, for everything that gets reported, we have to ask ourselves what didn't get reported. We always have to remember that even if a story is true, it's still a story. It isn't necessarily *the* story.

It's more important than ever to be informed and to think critically about the flood of information coming at us all the time. As we witnessed in Ferguson, getting it wrong puts lives, property, and communities at risk. The questions are: how do we make a judgment when we aren't there to see it for ourselves? How do we know the parts they aren't telling us? My sister said it well: "If the news says it's raining, I'm going to go outside now and make sure it's not just them, pissing in the wind."

Chapter Three

It's All about
the Optics

B efore the summer of 2014, I had never heard the term "optics" outside of an eye doctor's office. It didn't take very long, however, for optics to become the obsession of almost everyone around me. Simply put, "optics" is the new jargon, popular among politicians and media people, meaning "the way it looks." It's important to understand that while the media play a huge role in how things look, by determining what we see and how we see it, optics are tied more closely to our experiences and our personal biases and preconceptions. Sometimes the media try to force particular perceptions on us; more often, though, they subtly manipulate us by playing on our preconceptions.

I'll offer two very painful lessons about optics on the very day of the shooting. The first, as I've already discussed, was the fact that Michael Brown's body ended up laying in the middle of the street for almost four hours on a hot Saturday afternoon in August. This was not by design, but was sim-

POLICING FERGUSON, POLICING AMERICA

ply the result of circumstance. Recall that our forensics team was already at the scene of another incident. It's not only that they were an hour or so away, but even once they had arrived, their work took time. If I say that every commander understood the importance of being painstaking and methodical in the processing of this particular crime scene, it's not to imply that our police are generally careless or tend to cut corners in other cases. I'm simply making the point that on that Saturday, taking the time to do everything right, to leave no stone unturned, seemed to be the unspoken priority.

But as one of the public relations professionals who descended on Ferguson said later, it didn't matter what the reason was. It mattered *how it looked*. It was the first time I heard anyone say that explicitly. And how it looked that day was not good. Protest leaders said it was a public gesture of disrespect for Michael Brown and his family. It got worse. Some months after the shooting, at a roundtable discussion at Harvard University to which I had been invited, I was verbally attacked by a law professor from St. Louis. He claimed that I—not some vague reference to "the police," but I, specifically—had left the body in the street to intimidate, to let people know that they could be next. Presumably, he believed I was delivering a message to other young black men from the projects that if they disrespected the police, this was how they could end up. To this day, it pains me that anyone could think that.

The second major incident on the day of the shooting was the arrival of police dogs at the Canfield intersection, which I've mentioned. I can hardly imagine anything that could have looked worse on that hot and tense afternoon. This was a situation for which canine officers had trained and they were highly skilled, but the county police captain who had called for the dogs recognized immediately how terrible it looked, and how it ratcheted up the tension in the crowd. I saw it, too, and we managed to get the dogs called back and removed from the scene almost the minute they got there, but it was too late. In that brief moment, irreparable damage had been done to public perception and community relations.

Again, it didn't matter whether or not the canines legitimately or appropriately served the goal of public safety, the simple image of teams of mostly white police officers confronting a crowd of mostly black protesters with snarling dogs spelled disaster. It immediately conjured up memories of Selma and Little Rock and Bull Connor, and provided the first piece of ammunition for anyone who wanted to paint the police to be the dangerous aggressors, rather than the peacekeepers we believed we were.

This particular contradiction would play itself out dozens of times. Whenever the police would follow procedures or introduce certain kinds of tactical gear that were proven to save lives and protect property, we were pilloried for being aggressive or intimidating, for being the cause of the trouble rather than the response to it. Imagine the irony: if the police were the ones making all the trouble, who else, other than the police, was on hand to deal with that trouble after it started? Yet rational people seemed to believe that by becoming the aggressors, the police were somehow giving themselves a license to crack some heads, even if they were putting their own lives at risk to do so. And the idea of "optics" was at the root of it all, aided and abetted by the feverish media and rabble-rousing activists and politicians.

For example, one complicated but significant lesson in optics centered around the police use of tear gas as a means of crowd control. I'll get into the pros and cons of tear gas in a later chapter on policing practices, but in the context of optics, I just want readers to understand that police deploy tear gas with purpose, planning, and care. If a protest escalates into a riot, tear gas is a safe and effective tool for de-escalating violence. It is, without question, deeply unpleasant, and that's pretty much all the public understands about it. We don't use tear gas as an offensive weapon of attack, but only as a way to diffuse or disperse a large and violent crowd without injuring citizens. When a crowd is transforming into a mob—that is, when weapons are brandished, rocks and bottles are thrown, fires are being set, and masses of people begin to form into vocal or agitated groups that appear ready to do battle—police have a limited number of options. Moving in for physical confrontation or pointing weapons at citizens doesn't fit anybody's definition of "keeping the peace." Deploying tear gas can scatter a crowd and diffuse the momentum of a crowd about to rampage. While gas is painful to the eyes and lungs, the idea is to reduce the possibility of bloodshed.

Moreover, our practice is to never use gas without first issuing a warning and giving people time to get themselves out of the area and clear of the gas. That was the practice on those tense days in Ferguson, and it leads us to why tear gas became a part of the "optics" discussion. As I've said, the public heard endless descriptions of the "peaceful protesters" out on our streets. The narrative persisted despite the obvious facts on the ground. At the same time, tear gas exists in our collective unconscious as a weapon of oppression, conjuring up images of noble protesters and activists from the civil rights and Vietnam eras being manhandled by faceless, battle-ready police. So the mere mention of tear gas played into the assumed narrative. And, it gave the protest spokesmen and spokeswomen an easy target for complaint. I can't even count the number of discussions I had—with local and state politicians, reporters, activists, protest leaders, law enforcement officials from other agencies, and even representatives of the US Department of Justice—that centered on the use of tear gas.

The argument over tear gas played a role in another prominent episode having to do with optics. Michael Brown's death instantly became a matter of race—a young black man gunned down by a white policeman—having nothing to do with the actual circumstances of the shooting. As such, from the very beginning, the protesters in the street were overwhelmingly African American, while the police officers trying to keep a lid on the situation were mostly white. I'll get into the challenges of hiring minority officers in the next chapter, but it was an unavoidable fact that contributed to the optics problem in a big way, and became a huge point in the larger case against police in America.

Missouri governor Jay Nixon recognized how bad the optics were, and so four days after the shooting, he moved to replace the white law enforcement commanders on the scene. He chose Ron Johnson, a captain from the Missouri State Highway Patrol, to supervise police activity at the scene of the protests. Neither Nixon nor anyone else ever explicitly said that Johnson was chosen because he's African American. They claimed it was because he was from the area, or he was "comfortable with the community." Surely it wasn't because experience at the highway patrol made him an expert at crowd control or quelling an armed mob explicitly threatening harm to people, property, and police. Nixon had already been publicly critical of the efforts of local and county police, and apparently thought that a black commander like Johnson could help calm the crowd. Even worse, having this commander parachute in at the governor's order was tantamount to a vote of no-confidence in the officers already on the scene, undermining the authority of the men and women putting themselves on the line.

From the start, Johnson played the part of the savior, the man who was going to right the ship. Right off the bat, he started showing up at anti-police protest rallies. At one point, he told me that he didn't even think he and I were on the same side. He wanted to represent the "good police," as opposed to the oppressive storm troopers already at the scene. Jon Belmar and I were never officially relieved of command, but Governor Nixon, who hadn't bothered to contact either of us, called a press conference at which he introduced Ron Johnson and asserted that he would immediately stop using tear gas at the protests.

The experienced officers on the scene knew instinctively that there was little probability of keeping that promise, and sure enough, things got so out of hand on the streets of Ferguson that Captain Johnson ordered the use of tear gas on his very first night in command. In his press statement the following morning, however, he described it as a "calm" night. He said there had been no incidents, no injuries, and no tear gas; that it had been a night of peaceful protest.

At roll call that morning, officers shouted at the captain, "You lied!" They knew the real story: the seething crowds had thrown bricks, one striking an officer, and when they started overturning cars, tear gas had to be used. Trying to claim otherwise, Johnson lost his authority with officers at the outset. They literally shouted him down at roll call the morning after the first night. Seasoned officer, Lieutenant Colonel Michael Dierkes, had to step in.

What nobody anticipated was that the protesters would see right through Nixon's obvious pandering. Johnson kept upping the ante, calling press conferences at which he demanded Darren Wilson be indicted and that I resign. He went so far as to declare, at a rally in support of Michael Brown, "I wear this uniform and I should stand up here and say that I'm sorry." He won the hearts of the crowd while deepening the divide between the protesters and police and at the same time alienating every officer under his command. The irony was that when protesters would rush the police, and get right in their faces, screaming at them, threatening to rape their wives and kill their babies—which happened night after night after night—they saved their worst abuse for the black officers, adding accusations like "traitor," "house nigger," or "heel-licking nigger." In fact, this taunting got so deeply under Ron Johnson's skin that at one point he snapped. Someone in the crowd captured him on a cell phone video yelling back at the protesters, "You're punks! You're all punks!" Of all the cops on the scene for all those weeks, Johnson was the only one I knew of who lost his cool like that.

Ron Johnson took an enormous amount of abuse in Ferguson, although the public never saw any of that. People only ever saw what the people pointing the cameras chose to show them, which was Johnson, the good guy, standing arm-in-arm with the protesters, and me, the bad guy, standing with a line of cops in "battle dress." Jay Nixon couldn't really handle the optics of removing Johnson when it became clear that he could not effectively lead, but the governor eventually created a "joint command" that included the reinstated Jon Belmar, Mike Dierkes, and others.

I quickly learned that we could count on the media to highlight and exaggerate the optics of a particular situation, regardless of whether those optics were valid. So much of what we had to cope with in the months after Michael Brown's shooting could be traced to popular misconceptions, optics, media distortion, or more often than not, a combination of all three. Tear gas was no exception. I recall one episode involving Missouri state senator Maria Chappelle-Nadal. Despite our constructive interactions in the past, she chose to publicly denounce me and the Ferguson police, and became a vocal rabble-rouser, as if she were determined to prolong the trouble in our town.

Chappelle-Nadal was present one night when the crowd had gotten violent enough to warrant the deployment of tear gas. She was quoted the next day, describing the episode. "We were peacefully sitting. . . . I'm the senator for the area, and I felt threatened." When I spoke to the press, I tried to explain the rationale for using tear gas when a protest escalated toward violence, and how we made sure to warn people in advance so that everyone would have the option of getting away from both the potential mob violence and the adverse short-term effects of tear gas. "It's a crowd," I said. "If the crowd is getting violent, and you don't want to get violent, get out of the crowd." It seemed a simple, straightforward point. Take responsibility for yourself and for the situation.

And yet, this was a newspaper headline the next day: "Ferguson Police Chief: If You Get Tear-Gassed, It's Your Own Fault." I was outraged, but I can't say I was shocked. One article went on to quote a reporter who had been present that same night. "Somebody did throw a bottle or something off one of those trucks," he began. "But I didn't hear any gunfire. I didn't see any Molotov cocktails, any rocks being flung." The climate had become so poisoned that people were ready to assume the worst about the police, in this case that we were just itching for the chance to gas a crowd of innocent, peaceful people, and jumped at the opportunity presented by one broken bottle. I wanted to ask that reporter, and every know-it-all critic, did they want to be the one having to make that call night after night? Did they want to take on the responsibility of deciding what was a raucous but harmless demonstration and what was a dangerous situation in which people were likely to get hurt? We had crossed over some line. The public's default assumption was that the police were looking for opportunities to assert authority, to intimidate citizens in order to control them. I could talk until I was blue in the face about how the last thing police wanted was to stir the pot, to trigger confrontation, to put people further at risk. I could go on about our responsibility to protect the public's right to assemble and protest while also protecting their safety. But none of it mattered. The public had made up its mind, and there was nothing we could do to change perceptions.

The deployment of tear gas was one of many police tactics that came under fire from the press and the public. People condemned our protective gear, our vehicles, the barriers put on streets, even the number of officers on scene. Pundits on national television were going on and on about the "militarization" of police, while on the ground in Ferguson, we saw it as quite the opposite. Commanders would actually say things, "Hey, it's not like we're at war here," when we were trying to figure out how to keep people safe. Our goals were simple and clear: first, establish order, then diffuse tension and disperse violent groups, and always, always, make sure nobody got hurt. I believe that virtually all of the anger resulted from optics—from people misunderstanding the nature of police tactics and equipment, a problem made worse by distorted and sometimes even biased media coverage, and by protest leaders out to make a name for themselves. A later chapter devoted to policing will address these issues.

I realized fairly early on that the optics nearly always worked against me. It also became apparent that I would never be able to control the optics. While I would have to remain conscious of them at every minute, I could not let appearances stop me from doing my job. I've described the first press conference fiasco where I gave in to the public relations advisors who provided a script, and how the media picked up on my tics and mannerisms rather than on the information provided. It would be impossible to list all the times that the story became about me rather than the actual events. That same PR guy, who told me that the way things looked was all that mattered, advised me to stop talking to the press, making the case that anything I said or did would be used against me, and by extension, against the town leadership, the police, anyone in authority. I hadn't believed the consultant at first, but this kind of attack went on nearly every day. Still, my instinct told me that avoiding the press was a terrible idea.

Other police chiefs I knew had been through this kind of thing before and offered their guidance. I was gratified to receive help and support from the national leadership of National Organization of Black Law Enforcement Executives (NOBLE), in particular Chuck Ramsey, former chief of police in Washington, DC, and police commissioner for Philadelphia, and Cedric Alexander from DeKalb County, Georgia, outside of Atlanta, and the national president of the organization. A friend and colleague, Ken Gregory, the president of the state chapter of NOBLE, had contacted the national group, and urged them to do what they could for a brother officer he considered one of the good guys. These men were indeed noble to stand by me in the highly charged atmosphere of the Ferguson riots. They came to town with a group of police chiefs, from Cincinnati, Ohio, and from Sanford, Florida, where Trayvon Martin had been shot, and other cities.

Ramsey had lived through his share of media firestorms, and he advised me to never stop talking to reporters. He described the press as a "junkyard dog." "If you don't feed it," he said, "it's gonna go through your trash." His experience mirrored mine, and confirmed my instinct, which had been to make myself constantly available to the press, answer as many questions, and provide as much information as possible without jeopardizing any investigations or legal proceedings. Cedric Alexander even organized a meeting that included Ron Davis, the director of the Office of Community Oriented Policing Services at the Department of Justice, and other law enforcement officials and community leaders. Alexander also invited journalists from CNN so that the press might understand that our goals were to get everybody—the public, the police, the politicians—on the same page, so that we could de-escalate and resolve the situation without destroying the community. The input of those seasoned professionals, along with my experience of this meeting, which was marked by honest conversation and genuine listening, confirmed my intuition that the best thing I could do was to remain open and available to the press.

Ironically, the chiefs all seemed to agree on one point— that the press had a short attention span and would likely forget about Ferguson pretty quickly. That had been the case for many of them. They'd experienced riots or other problems that had been short-lived and that, like most new stories, just faded out of the spotlight. Of course, as time would tell, that didn't happen in Ferguson. Once we were about a week into the crisis, we all understood we were in uncharted waters.

For much of the time, it felt as if the optics were focused primarily on me. If the story was that a blameless gentle giant had been killed in cold blood, then the world needed somebody to blame. As far as the public was concerned, justice couldn't come down fast enough or hard enough on Darren Wilson, but as time went on and Wilson still hadn't been clapped in irons, people turned their attention to the next logical target—me. I was Darren Wilson's boss, the man responsible for putting him out on the street in uniform. More importantly, people began to believe that it was because of me and my "protection" or whatever "cover-up" I was orchestrating that he remained at large. As the white guy in uniform most often on camera, either at the scene of the protests or in interview settings, I became the symbol of the aggressive and oppressive policy. Amid all the calls for justice and equality and all the rhetoric about whose lives matter and brutality, the one constant refrain had only to do with me. Chief Jackson had to go.

I'm not naive. I get why people felt that way. Nobody had the patience to wait for the wheels of justice to turn. Something had to happen, the world needed to see somebody taking some kind of corrective action, regardless of whether there was actually anything meaningful anyone could do in that moment. Getting rid of the chief was an obvious move, and certainly that had happened in most cities that had gone through anything like this. It would have been an empty gesture, as it so often is when somebody loses their job in the wake of a scandal or crisis, but too many people believed it somehow represented "taking action."

Why didn't the town simply fire me? First, they believed in me. but it also happens that there are laws on the books in the state of Missouri that severely restrict the ability of mayors and town managers or councils to remove police chiefs. These laws came about in response to earlier incidents of chiefs losing their jobs because of local political squabbles rather than their actual performance on the job. The intent was to create fairer working conditions as well as to insure stability in law enforcement.

So it was up to me to step down, and while I knew that my departure was inevitable, I also knew I couldn't responsibly just walk away. I believe in the idea that people in positions of authority bear responsibility for the actions of those under them, but, to begin with, there was no actual evidence of any wrongdoing by Darren Wilson or anyone in our department. Moreover, I felt the responsibility of standing by the people under my command. To turn my back in such a difficult time, when every member of the Ferguson Police Department was risking his or her life every night to protect the town and its people, would have been an absolute betrayal of their trust, their loyalty, and their dedication. I can't imagine a leader setting a worse example. Talk about optics; these are the optics I cared about.

The people calling for my head lacked the foresight to understand that my departure at the height of the crisis would have created so many more problems than it would have solved. For starters, it would have demoralized the department at the worst possible time, something that could have rippled through the other law enforcement agencies. Then, of course, there was the question of who would replace me? I couldn't imagine anybody wanting to step into that mess with the eyes, and cameras, of the world focused on them. And yet, day after day, somebody or other turned up in the press somewhere, asking why I still had a job. I made it clear to people that I intended to see this thing through, to stay with the ship until it was righted.

It wasn't only the crowds on the street calling for my head. High-level political figures, including our governor, and at least one of our US senators, added their voices. Governor

Jay Nixon made it clear early on how much he would appreciate my resignation. Nixon, of course, had been plagued by optics all along, most notably when he called up the Missouri National Guard and ordered them into Ferguson in the early days of the rioting. It was not necessarily a bad tactical decision at the time, with busloads of protesters unloading onto the streets of town every day and increasing levels of street violence and destruction. The local law enforcement personnel on hand were at risk of being overrun, and the back-up made sense. The governor, however, didn't consider the optics of hundreds of soldiers descending on Ferguson. The media tore him apart, describing the initial National Guard deployment as the governor calling out "the army" to fight against "the people" or "our people." It was a public relations fiasco, and he quickly recalled the Guard, which accomplished little other than leaving the police on hand that much more vulnerable.

Would Nixon use the Guard in a cynical manner at a critical moment later, essentially holding the soldiers as a bargaining chip to compel my resignation? It is important to note that in the case of Governor Nixon, optics mattered in ways most people couldn't see. Nixon was a real comer in the Democratic Party, and there was much talk of his being groomed for bigger things. Both politicians and journalists I knew and trusted all believed that Hillary Clinton's organization was considering putting Nixon on the national stage, even as a potential running mate, and were letting him know what kind of optics they were looking for out of leadership. That man had a lot on the line, but when it was all over, his moment had passed. The consensus verdict on his performance that summer was clear. On the sign outside a Ferguson tire store, the ad for that week's sale was replaced with lettering that proclaimed: EPIC FAIL. JAY NIXON. EPIC FAIL.

Much more disappointing to me was the reaction of Claire McCaskill, the Democratic senator from our state. The senator and I knew each other, having worked together on certain initiatives in the past. She had been a prosecuting attorney and state auditor. We saw eye-to-eye on law enforcement issues that mattered deeply to me, and I believed I had earned her respect. When things got really hot, though—when the town and the state were caught in the crosshairs of national attention—it sure seemed to me that the senator wanted me thrown under the bus.

Early on, there were a series of meetings that included, at various times, Senator McCaskill; the state attorney general, Chris Koster; Bob McCulloch, the prosecuting attorney, Mayor Knowles, and John Shaw representing Ferguson; and representatives of the governor's office, of St. Louis County, and the city of St. Louis. The angry crowds on the street in Ferguson wanted someone held accountable for Michael Brown's death. At that meeting, Mr. Shaw was urged to terminate Darren Wilson's employment by our department, or at least to convince him to resign, but that was an absolute nonstarter as far as I was concerned. Wilson hadn't been convicted of anything; he hadn't even been charged with a crime. Still, there had to be a scapegoat, and all eyes eventually fell on me.

I vividly remember the phone call I received from Claire McCaskill, in which she turned up the pressure on me.

"Tom," she said, "you really need to step down." I asked her why that was, and her response was, to me, the very definition of optics. "You haven't done anything wrong. But we have to start over with a clean slate."

I asked, "Start what over with a clean slate?" and the senator answered only, "We just need to start over." McCaskill made it clear that my stepping down would look good to the people who were looting and burning our community, essentially making it clear that they needed to feed me to the lions. She ended the conversation by reiterating that I had done nothing wrong, but reminding me that "sometimes, you just need to fall on your sword." Immediately after we spoke, the senator went on radio and publicly said the same thing, that it was time for me to resign.

In these meetings with all the relevant local, state, and federal politicians, there was always a lot of talk about all the great things people were going to do for Ferguson—grants and other money for rebuilding, new business development, and so on, but the caveat was always made clear. It was all contingent on my resigning. I have to say it's possible that only made me dig my heels in. I asked Chris Koster, the attorney general, why the caveat was necessary. Why impose that price? If these were the right things to do for Ferguson, and if it was in their capacity to do them, why not just go ahead and do them? Crickets—no response. Needless to say, none of that money they talked about ever materialized.

The organizers of the meetings planned a big press conference where they would announce my resignation but at the same time lay out all these big plans for Ferguson, but one person in attendance, Lacy Clay, the United States congressman representing the district that includes St. Louis and Ferguson, said straight out that he refused to be the only black person involved in the press conference. Clay had hit on something valid and important; there were so few African Americans in positions of authority in this situation. But that wasn't his real problem; the issue for him was optics. He didn't want to get up there with all these white politicians looking like he was there for appearances' sake, like Ron Johnson had been.

The most glaring—and upsetting—example of optics rearing its ugly head came up in a meeting called by Ron Davis from the Department of Justice in the days before the decision of the grand jury regarding Darren Wilson's indictment was to be announced. My problems with the behavior of the DOJ in Ferguson are deep and thorny, so much so that I am devoting an entire chapter to them, but Davis's bold and foolhardy concession to optics at that critical moment in particular sticks with me. His purpose in calling the meeting, in fact, was to instruct all the law enforcement officials to consciously "control the optics" when the streets erupted in the inevitable demonstrations once the verdict was announced. Specifically, Davis instructed us not to use tear gas, making the argument that tactical tear gas "incites" people. We asked him outright if he understood that he was telling us to put officers at risk, for the sake of appearances, but he stuck to his position. He even went so far as to suggest we let the rioters take over the police station to give them a victory.

Everyone I've spoken to who attended that meeting agrees that it was nothing short of surreal. Here was a federal law enforcement official instructing police to put optics ahead of officer safety and sound police tactics. The story of that particular moment in the Ferguson narrative is complex and painful, as readers will see later, but for now, just think about how upside-down things had become. A representative of the highest authority in the country had traveled from Washington to tell a roomful of career police officials to set aside what they considered best for public safety in order to make sure everything looked right for the press and the public.

Chapter Four

All Roads Lead to Ferguson

P rotesters—and rioters—streamed into Ferguson for
weeks. Sheriff David Clarke of Milwaukee County put
it this way: "Groups started converging on Ferguson
like vultures on a roadside carcass." The bigger the crowds,
the more attention from the media, and the more play the
protests got in the media, the more the whole thing attracted
people to the town. And as long as the cameras kept rolling
and the spotlight remained focused on Ferguson, the more it
became a national platform for whoever wanted to exploit it.

As the demonstrations were taken over by more and more
outsiders, the whole crisis had less to do with Michael Brown
or Ferguson or me and our police department. While law
enforcement investigated what appeared to be the shooting of a man who had violently attacked a police officer, the
demonstrations quickly became about a culture of racial
injustice and police brutality. Of course, those issues need to
be front and center, but they were only indirectly connected

to what happened in Ferguson and should not have pushed aside equally important issues like institutionalized poverty, substandard education, housing, unemployment, and community breakdown. At any rate, anyone who wanted to talk in front of a national television audience about "a new civil rights movement" or a "war on the Black community by the police" found their way to Ferguson that summer.

There were plenty of what you might call the usual suspects. The Reverend Jesse Jackson came to town and led marchers down West Florissant Avenue, and described Michael Brown's death as a "state execution." He stood in front of the Ferguson police station making the "hands up, don't shoot" gesture. The welcome for Reverend Jackson wasn't quite as warm as some would expect. He got a lot of grief from protesters for using his time in Ferguson to ask for donations for his church. Some protesters approached Jackson on the street and lashed out at him for being a sell-out and an opportunist. He made a hasty exit from Ferguson but participated in "hands up, don't shoot demonstrations" in other cities.

Jesse Jackson caught heat in the national media as well. Ironically, it was CNN's Don Lemon, who had been less than fair with me, who took Jackson to task and provided some thoughtful context. In an interview, Lemon chastised Jackson for his failure to forcefully condemn the rioting and violence in Ferguson, and instead excusing it all as a gesture of pain. "I don't think anyone is in agreement with what played out," Lemon said, as he praised "the good people of Ferguson," and confronted Jackson with the idea that burning down stores that provided jobs and sustained neighborhoods, stealing from people, or destroying property had not advanced the cause of urban reconstruction. He also made the point that people on the street couldn't reasonably argue that justice hadn't been done, solely because justice didn't provide the results they wanted.

Another self-appointed leader and activist, the Reverend Al Sharpton, also met with a chilly reception. As much as the crowds in Ferguson got wrong, they were smart enough to see through some of the more obvious attempts to grab attention. Sharpton did get a lot of positive press coverage for a fiery speech he made in a Ferguson church, during which he made a number of false and inflammatory claims about what the investigation would reveal. To be fair, Sharpton did at least include a call to end the looting and burning, but it was brief and muted enough that it didn't get in the way of his fire and brimstone. He turned tail almost as quickly as Jesse Jackson, though, after members of the local clergy got on him for being a self-interested media hog, deflecting the attention away from Michael Brown and the Brown family in order to pontificate about race in America.

These were ideal examples of what Sheriff Clarke meant when he said of the people converging on Ferguson, "Instead of coming in to help and restore calm, [they came] to pour gas on that fire with some of the inflammatory and irresponsible rhetoric."

It was interesting how, before things got completely out of hand, the Ferguson protests attracted the established voices of the racial justice movement in America. Local figures like Anthony Shahid, a St. Louis-based activist for racial justice with whom I had developed a rapport, played a very prominent role in the days right after the shooting. Shahid typified the protest tactics of the old guard, interrupting news conferences or organizing marches and rallies and other forms of political theater that could be caught on camera and reported in the press.

Leaders from the Black Panthers and the Nation of Islam came in and, four days after the shooting, made a public event out of issuing an informal "cease-and-desist" order regarding the use of tear gas by police. Zaki Baruti represented what was called Universal African Peoples Organization, the vestiges of militant organizations from forty or fifty years ago. A separate organization, called the New Black Panther Party for Self-Defense, also tried to make its presence known in Ferguson; two of its members are currently in prison for plotting to use bombs to kill both me and the county prosecutor, Bob McCulloch. These New Black Panthers might have been the most determined of the people out to harm me. But they weren't the only ones by any means. Death threats became such a common part of my life that Mary Simmons, my executive assistant at the police station, began screening all my mail and all my phone messages and removing them all before I had a chance to read them.

I've heard it said that crises give us the chance to be our best selves. The crisis that fell upon us in Ferguson gave many people around me that chance. Their rising to meet this challenge was a bright spot, and not only because it provided the only moments of sanctuary I felt for months. My two brothers, Dan and Bob, had been very upset about the character assassination and abuse I was taking. They felt helpless and at a loss for something to do until the threats started coming in.

It became known through social media that protesters planned to come to my house, but when the death threats began (and there were hundreds), my brothers took action. The police were already giving my house extra patrol and even had an officer assigned to my street when the threats began. Reporters had already come to my door and tracked down my children. Dan and Bob were both former cops with military backgrounds. Dan had been a drill sergeant and Bob holds a black belt in tae kwon do. They decided to guard my house at night, when assaults were most likely to take place.

One night, I came home and found them, along with several friends, sitting in the yard in lawn chairs. My brothers had brought with them cops, ex-cops, former military and intelligence people, government contractors, and on and on. They were there every night until the threats ebbed. The regulars included my neighbor and friend Dane (he never could tell me what he actually did for a living), Mike (who taught me to fly decades ago), Del (who spends most of his time in the Middle East training soldiers and whatever else), and my nephew Andy (former military special ops). Other volunteers, people I knew and many others I didn't, started coming in on a daily basis. Their very presence turned around many a would-be arsonist or vandal. I was honored, and to this day wonder if I'll ever be able to properly thank them.

That first night, it was very late when I got home, but I tried to hang out and chat with the guys in front of my house. Dan put a stop to that, saying, "We're here so you can rest, so go inside and get some damn sleep."

I thanked them and started to walk inside when Dane said, "You know what you have to worry about tonight?"

"What?" I said.

"Not a fucking thing."

Several weeks into the crisis, Zaki Baruti arranged for a secret meeting I attended to ask for help restoring some order to the demonstrations. They were concerned—rightly so—that the protests had fallen into the hands of a younger generation who seemed to endorse aggression and random violence. Not much of substance came out of that meeting.

The late Dr. Akbar Muhammad, a leader of the Nation of Islam and a son of Elijah Muhammad, arrived amid rumors that Louis Farrakhan himself might soon follow. Our meeting was cordial, bordering on friendly. At the end, he asked me to clear up a rumor. "Is Darren Wilson your son-in-law?" he asked. I could only laugh and tell him no.

A group of leaders came together for a meeting in anticipation of the press conference at which I planned to release the video of Michael Brown robbing the convenience store and the name of Darren Wilson. A list of that meeting's attendees speaks volumes about how this tragic incident of street violence had become entirely about race. Adolphus M. Pruitt, head of the state chapter of the NAACP was there, as well as Gil Ford, the national president. I had known Ford since we had offices across from each other when I was the drug taskforce commander for St. Louis County Police Department. Representing the ACLU was Reddick Hudson, a former cop whom I also knew. There were also two representatives of the Department of Justice's Community Resources Service. There were no advocates for anything not directly related to racial equality.

Even though several of those present at that meeting had known me for years and were familiar with Ferguson, I had to explain the many positives about our work to the outsiders who had inserted themselves into the process. I went through all the awards and citations for the town and the police department, our initiatives to try and hold the apartment owners in Ferguson responsible for conditions there, and so on. I actually felt like I made some progress and provided some much-needed perspective, but looking back, I was probably kidding myself.

Not quite three weeks after the shooting, Akbar Muhammad and Zaki Baruti organized a meeting to plan for what they expected to be a huge rally on the streets of Ferguson. They told us to plan for one hundred thousand marchers, and so we organized tents, shuttle buses, a stage, and other accommodations. The meeting was cordial and polite, so much so that our visitors commented that I was nothing like how I was being portrayed in the press. No kidding. Bishop Giovanni Johnson ("Bishop G"), a helpful and collaborative local clergyman and organizer, even suggested that I march with the protesters, which was especially ironic, given that they'd already told us they'd be demanding my resignation at the rally. It wasn't the only time I helped groups of demonstrators organize what I started to call "anti-me" rallies, but I still had to read in the press about how my department stifled protest and stomped all over the First Amendment. Dr. Muhammad assured us that the event would be peaceful, that the Nation of Islam does not permit violence at its events.

Of course, nothing ever turns out like we plan. In the end, only about two thousand people showed up for this event, as opposed to the hundred thousand they had anticipated. More importantly, the march turned out to be anything but peaceful. Almost as soon as the speeches were completed, the organizers completely lost control of the crowd. Something like a thousand protesters went on a rampage, taking over some of the streets and finally storming the police station. We immediately called for help, established a protective line of officers in front of the building, and endured a tense standoff that lasted for several hours. The protesters put themselves nose to nose with the officers standing guard, screaming about raping their wives and daughters and threatening to "kill [their] grandbabies." The black officers again were singled out for particularly ugly abuse. At one point, somebody got in Captain Ron Johnson's face and called him a "black bitch," which nearly put Johnson over the edge. We had determined in advance to try and make few, if any, arrests, but Johnson suddenly wanted to start arresting everybody in sight. Fortunately, cooler heads prevailed.

I believe that the Nation of Islam was sincere about promising nonviolence at the event, which is one reason I don't believe that the rampaging protesters that day had anything to do with them. The organizers had brought their people in on buses, and cleared them out quickly, before things got out of hand.

The Nation of Islam had no presence in Ferguson prior to that summer, and I was surprised to find them showing up all of a sudden. The mosque just outside of Ferguson, with an entirely African American congregation, had already come forward as a calming force. The imam had even invited me to meetings there to promote community relations. The Nation of Islam was just another group showing up to exploit the free publicity in Ferguson to promote itself. This is not to say that the issues that any organization wanted to air were trivial or secondary. But with so many different people competing for airtime on our streets, it started to feel like they were all there to promote themselves, like somehow, all these individuals and groups were jockeying for position, trying to take the reins as the main voice of the African American community. I would never presume to speak for that community, but my sense, from talking to Ferguson's own clergymen and community leaders, is that they weren't happy about all these outsiders throwing their weight around and fighting a fight that wasn't theirs to fight. The impression I had was that these local clergy were particularly annoyed with figures like the Reverend Al Sharpton, who swooped in to put his stamp on the proceedings, while they were working around the clock to help manage the situation. It was as if they wanted to say, "Thanks, Al, but we got this."

With only a few notable exceptions, the men and women of the cloth who made their presence known during the protests took their roles as "shepherds" very seriously, constantly working with protest organizers and with police and other officials to keep the peace. The clergy seemed to understand that violence and bad behavior would drown out the voices of the protesters and overshadow any message they wanted to convey. My deputy chief Al Eickhoff and Bishop G came up with the idea of passing out orange "clergy shirts" to these people, so that they could be easily identified as a resource for protesters and police alike, but also to make it just a little easier to protect them if things got out of control.

Not everyone who descended on Ferguson left a bad taste in my mouth. Dr. Alveda King, a niece of Dr. Martin Luther King, former state legislator, activist, and author, was a truly well-intentioned visitor. King came to a meeting arranged by Kevin Jackson, a friend and local television personality, and brought Niger Innis, another prominent civil rights activist and the national spokesperson for the Congress of Racial Equality (CORE). Both King and Innis have spent their lives working for racial justice and equality. Dr. King arrived at the meeting with a long list of steps she believed we should take immediately to improve relations and ease tensions in Ferguson—more community outreach, diversity in hiring, school resource officers, programs for at-risk youth, and other ideas. We had long, frank discussions about her list while taking the visitors on a tour of the city, and we described the neighborhood associations we'd set up as well as the community newsletter, civic events, school programs, and other steps we had taken. We had a terrific, productive session together, at the end of which she told me how gratified she was to see that everything she had wanted to recommend was already in place in Ferguson. Again, I knew how much we were doing right in our town; I didn't know how to get that across to anyone in the middle of that crisis. Dr. King was one of the few visitors, if not the only one, who chose not to get up on a soapbox while she was in town. It had been a great meeting, but since there were no practical steps to take or statements to make as a result, she did not want it to be made public.

One by one, the big shots passed through Ferguson. There were the hip-hop stars like Flavor Flav and Killer Mike; politicians, including Ron Paul and Ben Carson; and intellectuals and pundits like Dr. Cornel West. As the professional football season began, a number of the St. Louis Rams players made a show of solidarity by saluting Michael Brown, displaying the "hands up, don't shoot" gesture before a game. It's fine for high-profile entertainment figures and athletes to express themselves on social issues, but to reinforce a lie is irresponsible. Jack Dorsey, cofounder of Twitter, came and marched alongside protesters. Dorsey did not seek publicity for his participation; as a native of St. Louis, he appeared to have a heartfelt concern for his hometown. It did seem bizarrely ironic, though, that Twitter was one of the main platforms for not only communicating and organizing the protests, but also for disseminating much of the misinformation that spiraled into hatred and violence.

At the same time, any number of grassroots organizations set up camp in Ferguson. We've already discussed the New Black Panthers, who often advocated violence. Much of the publicity attention focused on Black Lives Matter, an organization that most people immediately associate with Michael Brown and Ferguson. However, it actually had sprung up two years earlier after the shooting death of Trayvon Martin in Sanford, Florida. BLM's original mission had as much to do with gender equality and LGBT inclusion as with race, and it had existed as not much more than a social media hashtag before Michael Brown's death. After that, the group received a huge surge in supporters, added infrastructure, organized events, and gained real traction and momentum while many of its supporters advocated violence against police officers. As the organization asserted itself as one of the leading new voices in the racial justice movement, the very phrase, "black lives matter" became both a rallying cry, and hot-button debate issue. There was also the Organization for Black Struggle, founded in St. Louis in 1980 to address "the needs of the Black working class," according to its website. It's fair to say that the events in Ferguson in the summer of 2014 breathed new life into the group.

Some groups were actually created by those events, most notably the Don't Shoot Coalition and Hands Up United. Many of the protesters who had descended on Ferguson, apparently at random, were actually funded, at least in part, by larger national organizations, such as the Open Society Foundations founded and financed by George Soros. These groups are having varying degrees of success finding their footing amid all the other more established activist groups. Given the narrative so widely accepted by the public about what happened in Ferguson, it makes total sense that so many organizations would want to use the town as a platform. Some causes were worthy, and while I have no doubt that injustice does happen, and deserves all our attention, that didn't happen in Ferguson.

I met with any group or organization that was interested and willing to sit down, even if it was to ensure that the city could help plan a march or demonstration in a way that kept people safe. I figured out march routes, organized traffic-free protest zones, and even brought food and water to the truly peaceful protesters who gathered daily across the street from the police station. I had the feeling that anyone who would take the time to communicate with me and my officers would realize that we were working toward similar goals. I don't think this ever made it into the press coverage, but a group organizing the daytime protests actually circulated petitions urging the city to keep me from leaving my position.

One day, I was heading to lunch downtown with a colleague when a group of about twenty protesters came sprinting in our direction. As they passed, one of them slowed and turned and gave a friendly shout.

"Hey, Chief Jackson!"

I returned his greeting. "Hey! Where you guys running to?"

The man explained that there was a protest in support of Darren Wilson about to take place a few blocks away, and they needed to go stage a counterprotest.

"Okay, then, keep it peaceful!"

"Thanks, Chief! Don't let them make you resign!"

Moments like this perfectly captured how surreal the atmosphere had become in Ferguson. I had a similar experience some months before. My sergeant and I arranged to meet at the firehouse with some activists who had been organizing protests at the Ferguson Farmers' Market. As the meeting got started, one of them looked at me and paused.

"Hey, I know you . . . " He said. We worked out that he recognized me because I had been going door-to-door in his neighborhood not long before that, handing out information about a new community center that I had helped get off the ground. From the encounter, he had assumed nothing more than that I was another Ferguson resident trying to do something productive in town. "You never told me you were the police chief," he added, implying that if he had known I was the chief, his earlier assumptions would have been all negative.

Getting to know each other as people makes all the difference in the world. It is the very essence of "community policing," as far as I'm concerned, but we'll get to that in a later chapter. As for this particular activist, our paths were to intersect quite a lot. The organization he represented, the Peace Keepers, acted as an important ally to police, clergy, and city leaders in Ferguson, helping to maintain calm at critical moments. But later, when we shared the stage at a public symposium on policing, he brutally cursed me out in public. However, we managed to make amends after that confrontation, and his activism took on a very positive purpose.

Chapter Five

The Real Lives
of Cops

The image of the stereotypical hard-ass redneck police-man has been hammered into our brains by genera-tions of movies and television shows. Whether it's a big-city cop on the take or a cigar-chomping cracker police chief in the deep south declaring, "I'm the law in this town," Americans have become used to the idea that cops operate by their own rules, that if they aren't openly corrupt they all at least believe, somewhere deep down, that the law doesn't apply to them in exactly the same way it applies to every-body else.

When I first came on the job, more than thirty-five years ago, I ran into some of those guys, the old school guys who cursed the addition of two-way radios to patrol cars because they couldn't stand the idea of anybody in authority know-ing where they were and what they were up to at any given moment. These old guys got more bitter and angry as tech-nology got more sophisticated, having convinced themselves that all the new tools that were supposed to make them better at their job were actually keeping them from doing the job the way they thought it should be done.

And yes, there were veteran cops who liked throwing their weight around, who did actually think that being a cop entitled them to get rough with people, to show them who's boss. To be honest, I was attracted to the physicality of police work, but in the same way an endurance athlete is drawn to marathon races or Ironman events. Being a cop can be physically demanding, sometimes requiring strength, speed, and stamina, and I understand taking pride in that. However, in my view, being tough was always about what I could take; never for a second was it about what I could dish out.

When I took over as chief in Ferguson, I found that cleaning house is never as easy as you want it to be. I had a lot of hardworking and dedicated officers on the force, but as the press has never tired of pointing out, the racial and ethnic makeup of the Ferguson police force didn't match that of the town's population. I still cringe whenever I read about this, not because it's so obvious, but because it reflects such basic ignorance and willful blindness on the part of the press. It was as if the pundits and reporters believed that somehow this hadn't occurred to me, a white police chief in a predominantly African American city. That imbalance weighed on me, as it does every other police chief in every other similar community in America, and correcting it was a priority from my first day on the job. I promoted the first African American supervisors in Ferguson, and like all those other police chiefs, I would have given anything to have a pool of black candidates from which I could hire new officers. But guess what: that pool exists mostly in the public's imagination.

The number of African Americans coming out of the police academies around the country and the number applying to positions on municipal forces doesn't come close to matching the percentage of African Americans in the population. People can debate the reasons for that, but it seems pretty obvious to me that if you grow up thinking police are the enemy, if your parents and grandparents experienced police as the enforcers of Jim Crow laws and countless other indignities, you're not likely to be drawn to law enforcement as your ticket to the American Dream. Many young black men and women wanted nothing to do with police, and tended to look at peers who became cops as sellouts or worse. That point was driven home night after night during the Ferguson riots.

With young black candidates at a premium, the chances of luring them to a police department in a small town or city, especially one that's struggling economically and tightening its budget, are very slim. Bigger cities offer better salaries, as well as more glamor, and snap up those candidates right out of school. In fact, I did hire black rookie officers very early in my tenure at Ferguson, but I wasn't able to hang on to them. They quickly moved on to more lucrative opportunities elsewhere. And it's not like those big-city jobs were any less problematic. Years before, when I worked on drug and gang task forces in St. Louis, we had trouble recruiting black officers to work with us. I could understand why: word got around that they would be sent undercover where white cops would be immediately suspect. Not only were those the most dangerous assignments, but the officers started to feel like they were only recruited because of their color.

The public needs to understand that this problem is pervasive. The Ferguson Police Department got ripped to shreds by the press, and by the report issued by the US Department of Justice, because of the racial imbalance on our force. But the DOJ faced exactly the same problem; at the time of the troubles in Ferguson in 2014, there were no nonwhite agents in the St. Louis office of the FBI and, as far as I could tell, each and every one of the DOJ lawyers sent to "investigate" the Ferguson police and courts was either white or Asian.

A lot of buzzwords about policing get tossed around these days, often in ways that show little understanding of what the terms mean. You hear a lot about "broken windows" policing, "hot spot" policing, "stop and frisk," or everybody's latest holy grail, "community policing." These terms attempt to describe approaches to policing that, in practical terms, dictate how a department or municipality allocates resources. As happens with so many issues in the news, the media tend to discuss policing philosophies in black-and-white terms, as if we are able to choose one and stick with it, to the exclusion of all the others. Nothing could be further from reality. The world we live in is constantly changing; the needs of a town and the responsibilities of a police force differ from neighborhood to neighborhood, block to block, and incident to incident. Any law enforcement official who is paying attention taps into all of these and other strategies, often at the same time, in an effort to maintain a safe and livable community.

"Broken windows" policing focuses on minor quality-of-life crimes, with the goal of creating a general sense of order that prevents more serious crime from becoming the norm. The idea arose in the early 1980s out of an article by two social scientists, James Q. Wilson and George L. Kelling, that is often summarized in this way: "Consider a building with a few broken windows. If the windows are not repaired, the tendency is for vandals to break a few more windows. Eventually, they may even break into the building, and if it's unoccupied, perhaps become squatters or light fires inside."

In their article published in the *Atlantic Monthly* in 1982, Wilson and Kelling wrote:

> Serious street crime flourishes in areas in which disorderly behavior goes unchecked. The unchecked panhandler is, in effect, the first broken window. Muggers and robbers, whether opportunistic or professional, believe they reduce their chances of being caught or even identified if they operate on streets where potential victims are already intimidated by prevailing conditions. If the neighborhood cannot keep a bothersome panhandler from annoying passersby, the thief may reason, it is even less likely to call the police to identify a potential mugger or to interfere if the mugging actually takes place.

This approach was popularized first in New York City in the 1990s under Mayor Rudy Giuliani and his police commissioner, Bill Bratton. They had officers cracking down on public drinking, turnstile jumping in the subways, graffiti, other petty vandalism, and most famously, the city's notorious "squeegee men"—guys who ran up to cars stopped at intersections, cleaned the windshield, and then demanded a tip for their services. The goal was to clean up the city and make it the norm for people to respect each other and the law. People don't necessarily agree on the effectiveness of their approach. The streets did seem friendlier, but many argued that the improvements were only superficial, and that the policies were heavily biased against poorer (and primarily nonwhite) neighborhoods in the city.

In New York City, broken windows police tactics gave birth to the controversial practice known as "stop and frisk," in which police are empowered to stop individuals on the street and search them for weapons or contraband. I don't think anyone in the country was surprised when studies began to accuse the NYPD of bias in this practice. Young men of color made up the overwhelming majority of those detained on the street, particularly in high-crime neighborhoods. The practice was found to be unconstitutional by one court, but that decision is still being contested at the time of this writing.

Critics wondered if the resources allocated to stop petty street crime could have been used to improve the lives of people in those areas in more meaningful ways, such as job counseling, family services, education, or health resources. As we'll see, this is the kind of thinking that moves us toward "community policing."

Another strategy, "hot spots" policing, seems equally logical at first glance, but has likewise triggered a lot of criticism when put into practice. Hot spots policing is exactly what it sounds like—concentrating resources in areas with the highest crime rates. Policymakers tend to think of this as a *place-based*, as opposed to *people-based*, approach to law enforcement. Even when commanders are scientific about it, applying statistical data about the numbers of crimes or calls to police from specific areas when assigning their officers and resources, the results are likely to appear race-based. The reality of today's cities almost dictates that hot spots policing is going to make it look like police are actively targeting poorer neighborhoods of color for their crackdowns. Think about it—criminal activity is determined not by race, but by poverty, unemployment, lack of opportunity, and a weakened social fabric. And while there is plenty of white rural poverty in America, in our metropolitan areas, poverty frequently is concentrated in the public housing neighborhoods, often dominated by nonwhite and immigrant populations. If police chiefs follow the crime statistics, that's where we send our officers. So, yes, of course it looks like there's a greater police presence in those neighborhoods, and it's easy to see how it would look to the residents like a means of intimidation.

In Ferguson, both of these tactics came into play in the public housing neighborhoods, including the apartments near where Michael Brown was killed. These areas generated the majority of dispatch calls and were the scene of most of Ferguson's violent crimes. Many of those were drug-related, but plenty others were rooted in domestic conflict and abuse. There were three daytime shootings in the public housing apartments in my first few months on the job in Ferguson, plus numerous robberies and burglaries, purse snatching incidents, car break-ins, and the like. If the residents of a particular neighborhood are calling the police more frequently to request help maintaining peace and order, why wouldn't a police chief assign more resources in that neighborhood?

At the same time, there were more than enough opportunities to improve quality of life in the public housing areas with selective broken windows policies. The most obvious example would be what we came to call "vehicle challenges"— young people, more often than not African American males, walking or sometimes just standing in the middle of busy streets, refusing to move out of the way of car traffic. This relatively minor infraction became so commonplace in parts of Ferguson that it rose to the level of a significant public nuisance. Our department received daily calls of complaint, not just from people passing through on busy thoroughfares, but from the people who lived in those areas and couldn't get to their own homes or to jobs or stores because their own neighbors were in the way.

Vehicle challenges and other broken windows-type offenses continued to play a major role in Ferguson's troubles. We didn't haul people off to jail for blocking the street, but our officers certainly handed out tickets. They regularly wrote out other citations for things like derelict vehicles that cluttered up the area, unregistered and uninsured cars (many of which would be involved in the numerous traffic violations that were cited), and various disturbances of the peace. These are exactly the kinds of citations—generated in response to increased crime rates and specific requests for help from residents, and intended to instill respect for neighbors and community—that the Department of Justice would later use as evidence of institutional racism and abuse in Ferguson.

It's hard to argue with the data. Those tickets accounted for a lot of Ferguson police activity, way too much in my opinion, and looked even worse from the outside. People would ignore those small tickets, letting them pile up for months or years, until the city court would eventually issue a bench warrant. Of course, that only compounded the problem. (When I come to my detailed examination of the DOJ's wildly distorted report on Ferguson, I'll explain my efforts as chief to undo that piece of local culture.)

It would be logical at this point to ask what we could do—in fact what we did—to help bring out bigger-picture improvements in our city's poorer neighborhoods so that these kinds of daily crimes wouldn't seem like a young person's only alternative. This gets us to "community policing," every politician's favorite "big new idea." Of course, there isn't anything new at all about community policing. According to the US Department of Justice's own published literature, community policing is a policy by which police allocate resources in ways "that support the systematic use of partnerships and problem-solving techniques to pro-actively address the immediate conditions that give rise to public-safety issues such as crime, social disorder, and fear of crime." It seems simple and obvious: treat the disease, and the symptoms will resolve on their own. I assure you, it is neither simple nor obvious. It is absolutely the fondest wish of everyone in law enforcement. It may also be absolutely impossible, from a policing perspective.

The cop on the beat is a figure out of American folklore, from the friendly patrolman sitting side-by-side with a lit-tle boy at a neighborhood lunch counter, to the small-town sheriff out west, to *West Side Story*'s Officer Krupke, single-handedly trying to prevent a gang war in New York City. In our nostalgic imagination, a cop knew the people on his beat by name, and they knew him. That familiarity bred mutual respect. It's a really nice picture, but we shouldn't waste time longing for a piece of the past that may never have even existed.

In those mythical old days, police received a tiny frac-tion of the training they get today. If you accept the Justice Department's description of community policing at face value, and want police to address the conditions that give rise to public safety issues, then you're looking to cops to somehow address education, economic opportunity, hous-ing, childcare, health care, substance abuse and addiction, broken families—in short, the entire list of social ills that lead to poverty and crime. That's asking an unreasonable amount of any individual, but let me assure you, the police have not backed down from the challenge.

When I came to Ferguson I saw to it that every officer received special training in active listening, counseling, communications, crisis intervention, and de-escalation. All this was in addition to the standard training regarding use-of-force protocols, domestic violence intervention, and racial profiling. Our officers trained alongside mental health professionals to learn how to identify symptoms of mental illness. They worked together to create on-the-spot treatment protocols. The state of Missouri mandates cultural awareness training for police officers, but I went even beyond those requirements, bringing in community leaders, especially from the Muslim community, to foster a deeper conversation. Most of the cops on the Ferguson force were college-educated and approached their work as committed professionals. They loved the way this training empowered them.

Even if we all believed that the police should be able to do something about every bad condition in society, and even if we could provide all the training in the universe, we'd need more police. These days, people like to complain about the overwhelming police presence in America, but the fact is that there aren't enough cops on the street to make effective community policing a reality. The same economic factors that lead to poverty and high crime rates also lead to diminishing police resources. It's not complicated: a strong local economy generates local tax revenue, and that revenue funds things like schools, police, fire departments, and social services. As businesses close or leave town, people lose jobs, and then the loss of disposable income makes it harder for shops and other businesses to stay open, and things spiral downhill. Schools' staffs shrink and education suffers, leaving children unprepared for the challenges ahead. So, as the conditions that give rise to public safety issues get worse, police forces also shrink. There are fewer and fewer cops in the areas of America that need them most, regardless of your approach to policing. When I came on in Ferguson, we barely had enough officers to provide the most basic policing, let alone the host of social services suggested by community-policing advocates.

With all that as background, let me try to describe the life and work of the average police officer, particularly in Ferguson, Missouri, before, during, and after the troubles there. I've already described, at various points, the state of the Ferguson Police Department when I arrived and some of our efforts to improve it. We hired and promoted minority officers where we could, did what we could to purge the force of long-standing members who clung to outmoded and unhelpful attitudes. We modernized the equipment and training as much as the budgets would allow and took steps to integrate our officers into the daily life of the community.

Despite dwindling resources, we made real progress, helping establish and maintain nine different community associations, through which the public could work together with city leadership and police to improve conditions in individual neighborhoods. We had a lively and diverse community of citizen volunteers working with our department through our Volunteers in Police Service (VIPS) program, ensuring that even if I had trouble hiring and holding on to minority officers, people from every race and economic level were present in our headquarters every day, keeping us connected to their concerns and issues. The entire city leadership was involved in the Ferguson Youth Initiative (FYI), which established a variety of programs to specifically benefit African American youth. Working with the FYI and other community programs helped me personally, since I could deepen my own relationships with minority leaders, such as city council member Dwayne James, whom I considered a friend. Of course, all that changed almost overnight in the wake of the Michael Brown shooting.

Certain cops were designated "community resource officers," with a specific mandate to build relationships with the public and identify areas beyond traditional law enforcement concerns where the department and the city could add valuable assistance. In 2010, Ferguson was an All-American City Award finalist and won a civic award and received a monetary grant for a neighborhood program that reduced crime and improved quality of life. In 2014, Ferguson received an award from the International City/County Management Association for programs that promote the safety, health, and wellness of citizens. Many of our officers used their personal, off-duty time to visit and maintain a presence in the most challenged neighborhoods, like the public housing projects. The size of Ferguson's police department, as well as the physical layout of the town, make police foot patrols impractical, so our officers generally did their work in patrol cars. Spending time in neighborhoods while not on duty allowed for more direct personal contact. To build on that, we began arranging family days, in which the town would sponsor a fair or picnic with food and "resource displays"—firetrucks and other official vehicles and equipment—so children could come out, have some fun, get to know us, and see that none of that stuff was threatening. These events were successful, drawing lots of families.

Ferguson is a small town, with a small police force, and we did whatever we could to make that iconic image of the friendly neighborhood cop a reality. Our officers were not faceless enforcers, but men and women known by name and considered part of the fabric of the town. Personally, I made a point of being wherever things were happening in Ferguson, and just about everybody knew me. I sat on a variety of planning commissions around town and participated in all sorts of events, from singing the national anthem at various events to serving as parade marshal and kicking off public road races. I wanted our officers to understand the importance of taking an active role in the community.

One example of that involvement had special resonance for me. When we assessed the crime statistics in Ferguson, we saw that the highest concentrations of both petty crimes and more serious, sometimes violent, crime were in the neighborhoods dominated by public housing—Oakmont Townhomes, Park Ridge Apartments, Northwinds Apartments, Versailles Apartments, and Canfield Green Apartments, outside of which Michael Brown was shot. In the decade or two before I came on the job in Ferguson, the number of public housing projects there had grown very quickly, until low-income residents—most of them on some form of public assistance—made up a significant percentage of the town's population.

A lot has been written about public housing, a well-intentioned governmental effort that has, over time, created at least as many problems as it has solved. I'm in law enforcement, and while people seem to think I should also be an expert in social policy, I can only tell you what I've observed. I've met many hardworking residents in public housing, people working multiple low-wage jobs while trying to raise families and who see the projects as a temporary stopover on the way to a better life. But I've also come across many people who seem incentivized to remain part of the system, which is almost designed to look the other way, as if in providing housing and food subsidies the country didn't have to worry about failing schools and vanishing economic opportunity.

Many of the public apartment complexes in the area were physically falling apart, largely ignored by inattentive management companies working for absentee landlords who just sat back and collected federal subsidies. There was an enormous transient population, with large numbers of people essentially squatting in small apartments where nobody even knew whose name was on the lease. Women with children were hanging on to subsidized apartments while hiding their boyfriends from authorities, so that they could continue to collect assistance for single mothers. Residents who are gaming the system are not likely to be active in the community in a positive way.

Local, state, and federal agencies might have been better equipped, better trained, and sufficiently resourced to improve the state of the projects and their residents, but none did. However, working hand in hand with the city government, that's exactly what we did. We tracked down the owners of all the buildings, some of whom were living as far away as Boston, Massachusetts, and one by one, got them to enter into agreement with the city to clean up their properties. This went beyond completing long-neglected maintenance and repairs; it called on the owners to ensure that occupancy was in keeping with the housing code and the lease agreements, and to improve the quality of life in other ways. We also called on the owners to help the city bring down the crime rates by providing security guards and cameras throughout the apartment complexes. The hope was that through such measures, we could reassign resources away from the petty broken windows policing that was clogging up the justice system.

I'm not saying that this effort did anything to address the real underlying problem of concentrated poverty, but at the very least, it was one step toward making these neighborhoods more livable. I wanted every resident of Ferguson, regardless of economic circumstances, to be able to take pride in the town, the way I did. Our town had a long way to go, but we were heading in the right direction, with support from the residents. For all the public outcry about the city leaders being blind to the needs of our African American population, the record shows that both the police department and the civilian government had made those needs a priority. As far as I'm concerned, many of these programs were the very definition of community policing, and we were doing it long before the term became a national rallying cry.

It almost goes without saying that all the good work our department did building relationships in the community became largely irrelevant within a day or two of the shooting. (I gather that chiefs and departments had similar experiences after newsworthy events in other cities, such as Charlotte, North Carolina.) Maybe it's an indication of how fragile such relations really are, but they went out the window almost overnight. It's ironic that in the first couple of days, a good part of the local population stood ready to defend the department and expressed concern about the wave of trouble about to overtake the city. Residents were struggling to get to their own front doors through the crowds and the violence, and were coming to us for help, yet that all had to happen on the Q.T.; nobody wanted to do anything publicly that seemed to show trust in, or support for, the police. African Americans with whom I had long-standing friendships, whether they were private citizens who worked for the city or volunteered in our headquarters, or local politicians with whom I had worked productively, suddenly treated me like a stranger. This all made me more sad than angry. I understood that a lot of good people were caught up in a confrontation driven by those who knew nothing of Ferguson, and that had become much bigger than Ferguson.

The commitment of Ferguson's police officers, however, did not waver for a moment. On the contrary, facing a situation so far beyond anything they had ever experienced, our force had to redouble its efforts to protect the city and its people. Not only were they all working around the clock, they were doing so under conditions that grew increasingly more dangerous and agonizing by the hour. The trouble came not from actual Ferguson residents, who only wanted to get to their jobs and homes, but from outsiders, many of them brought there, and sometimes allegedly even paid, by activist organizations based elsewhere. Our job, of course, was to look after the people of Ferguson. This was a point I tried to make over and over, not just to county, state, and federal officials, but in press interviews as well. Nobody wanted to hear it.

This is exactly the point at which the rules and standards by which law enforcement normally operates started to get turned inside out. A simple example: one night, somewhere around midnight, protesters marched through a residential neighborhood, banging on drums or cans, shouting through bullhorns, illegally blocking traffic, and disturbing the peace. Anxious and feeling threatened, the residents of that neighborhood complained, and county officers made some arrests, for which they immediately took flak. Higher authorities—as well as some press and protest organizers—felt the police violated those protesters' rights to assemble and demonstrate. The police on the ground had to make a determination: were the nonresident protesters' rights worth more than the rights of the residents? As it turned out, the protesters had priority, at least in the court of public opinion. Officers and commanders faced this kind of decision, although usually on a larger scale, every day.

Now, it's important to point out that civil disobedience is a tried-and-true protest tactic, and it can be extremely effective. But civil disobedience is exactly what it sounds like: it's not legal. Protesters make a conscious decision to break the law, and to accept the consequences, in order to make a point and further a cause. In fact, police faced civil disobedience virtually all day, every day, for weeks on end in Ferguson and only acted against it when they felt a threat was real.

We faced similar criticism when police action appeared to stifle the protesters' right of free speech. The press and the public regularly failed to make the distinction between "free speech" and "unprotected speech." It's one thing for marchers to chant "End police brutality!" or "Fuck the police!" or "Get the police!" That kind of expression of generalized anger is protected, even if it appears to foment violence. But that's not the case when a protester walks up to a cop, gets inches from that cop's face, calls the cop *by name*, and screams, "I'm going to kill you! I'm going to find out where you live and kill your babies and fuck your wife!" There's a world of difference, from a civil rights perspective, between publicly challenging an institution of authority and making specific threats to an individual. That threat is not protected, and it absolutely justifies arrest. Even still, that kind of thing happened hundreds of times every day, and was mostly endured by the cops, without arrest. Again, we all had to make judgment calls, and there was simply no way to respond to each one of those threats.

At one point, the local cops, those who lived nearby and were concerned for the safety of their families, made the decision to remove their name tags from their uniforms. Ironically, by the time our officers made that decision, it was too late. The damage was already done, and once again, the main culprit was social media. Activists had cataloged the names of the officers on the street and then searched sites like Facebook, where these officers maintained a presence, for their personal information: where they lived, where they liked to hang out, the names of their spouses and their children, and so on. Where that information was protected by security settings, the activists were able to hack into the information. Those names and addresses were posted on social media for all the world to see. The Ferguson cops, most of whom lived either in town or very close, were terrified for their families, friends, and neighbors, and a good portion of them ended up moving away. Those officers who had a "take-home car"—a Ferguson patrol vehicle they were allowed to use to travel to and from work—were in even greater danger with this symbol of authority parked in front of their house, clearly marking them as a target. What had been considered a perk of the job, even a deterrent to crime, had become a dangerous liability.

As for the name tags, incredibly, representatives of the US Department of Justice objected to their removal, insisting that it was "unconstitutional" for officers to appear in public without identification and ordered that they be put back on. To this day, I am unable to find that clause in the Constitution.

It all but confirmed for me, at that moment, that our federal parent agency wasn't actually there to help. In fact, at one roll call attended by DOJ lawyers, they actually told my officers that as soon as they put on the badge, they forfeited their constitutional rights. It was typical of the DOJ's high-handed attitude toward local law enforcement, to attempt to intimidate us with official-sounding but nonsensical claims.

I would ask readers to put themselves in the position of the commanders on the ground during the demonstrations. There had been peaceful protests: vigils, speeches, sit-ins, and so on. But there had also been rioting, looting, burning, random gunshots, rock and bottle throwing, Molotov cocktails, over-turned cars, broken windows, and many other kinds of random vandalism and violence. The experience of the police during the demonstrations had been that "protest" could explode into "riot" almost instantaneously. Yet someone at the scene had to judge the exact moment when that line would be crossed. At any given moment, some exhausted cop would have to decide whether to let the protest ride, or intervene before somebody got hurt. We know now that it really didn't matter what decision that officer made; it would inevitably be second-guessed. And yet, I challenge anyone who wasn't there—any pundit, journalist, activist, or politician—to take the responsibility for that kind of decision. Which of the second-guessers would want to be the one to have said, "No, let's wait a little longer," only to see their inaction result in people getting hurt? This is exactly what law enforcement professionals get paid to do, and one hopes that the more experienced we are, the more nuanced our decision-making will be. The worst problem is that there can never be any way of proving that we made the right decision. You can't tell people, after the fact, about the injury and destruction that *didn't* happen because of the action you took. It's an impossible, no-win situation.

That decision-making process got even more difficult as the situation dragged on for weeks and weeks, with different commanders from different law enforcement agencies rotating in and out. For the rank-and-file officers on the street, that translated into inconsistency. On the first few nights, the guidelines were pretty cut-and-dried: violence erupted and police responded. As time wore on, though, the tactics of the protests evolved. At the same time, more commanders arrived from different places to help out. Of course, most of those officers were no more connected to Ferguson than the hundreds of protesters who had come from all over the country. More problematically, though, the different commanders would bring different levels of tolerance or engagement, different sensitivities, different strategies.

We saw this play out early on when Captain Ron Johnson took over command of the demonstration area. The "soft tactics" that he introduced, and which were intended to de-escalate the protesters' hostility, actually had the opposite effect. Seeing new openings, the protesters were emboldened, at one point almost overrunning the West Florissant command post, and eventually forcing Johnson to break his promise not to use tear gas. It made some sense for him to make a show of greater tolerance, but it also exposed the officers to more abuse and to heightened danger. At times, the whole scenario was further complicated by state or federal officials, who weren't necessarily on the scene and had their own agendas, sending orders down through the chain of command regarding police activity.

It was hard enough for the cops on the line, even without this complication. Most officers were putting in twelve-hour shifts, day in and day out. Commanders had to monitor the officers very carefully, cycling them out for time off, so that we didn't have to worry about people snapping under pressure.

The commanders themselves, all under similar pressure, had to keep an eye on each other's schedules, so that they could stay fresh and clear-headed. As a result, the ratio of commanders to rank-and-file officers was much higher than normal. Everybody understood the absolute necessity of a calm, well-rested force.

For all the abuse heaped on the Ferguson police throughout those months, it was really very heartwarming to see the dedication of the officers, their spouses, and their families. Some of the people I worked with are particularly worth singling out. Ferguson's lead dispatcher, Shannon Dandridge, along with her direct supervisor, Sergeant Mike Wood, had made themselves invaluable to the department well before the violence and unrest began. Shannon and Mike constituted the team who implemented and oversaw my mission of bringing the Ferguson PD up to date with cutting-edge communication and record management technology. (Ironically, the fact that we had just begun the complicated process of computerizing all our records meant that some of those records were in storage boxes, difficult to access, when the Department of Justice lawyers investigated our operation, allowing them to condemn us for sloppy records management.)

I had known Shannon since she was a sixteen-year-old "Police Explorer" with the county police department when I was a road sergeant there. Now grown up, she had become a communications officer (police dispatcher), married a city policeman, and started a family. I was delighted to see her when I first started at Ferguson PD, although it made me wonder where the years had gone. Mike and Shannon had taken on the task of implementing the new state-of-the-art custom public safety software, from Information Technologies, Inc. (ITI), a company based in St. Louis. We were going all in, with automated records management, court docketing, corrections, and CAD (computer-aided dispatch) platforms, and we were one of the first departments to switch to this company's systems.

It's important to understand what a giant task this would have been under normal conditions: implementation, conversion, customization, training, troubleshooting, maintenance, not to mention calming and cajoling the people who didn't like the idea of change. Mike and Shannon made it work during the major renovation of the police building already underway, and even through the riots and the invasion by Eric Holder's DOJ. When we started on this mission to become the most technologically up-to-date police department around, we had a vision of what the final product would look like. Mike and Shannon had the tough task of actually building that product. Fortunately, ITI president Dave Lommel assigned us a former state trooper turned techie, Drew Stewart, as well as my old friend and colleague, retired chief Carl Wolf, to guide us through the process. Throughout the daily riots, they stuck with us like family.

On top of all that, Shannon had taken on another mission. Along with Kelly, Angie, and the rest of the St. Louis Police Wives' Association, she gathered volunteers and donations to organize a meal stop and safe place for the hundreds of officers and support staff who came to face the angry mobs and violent protesters on a daily basis. They provided three meals a day and a brief escape from the vulgarity and abuse heaped upon the cops by what the press called "peaceful protesters." As the donations and volunteers poured in, their refueling station soon outgrew the space that businessman Mike Lonero had graciously made available. Before long, we had two meal stops occupying space at the two command posts, one on West Florissant Avenue and the other at the

made a regular practice of trying to communicate face-to-face with pro-sters. Here I'm walking alone and protected into a nighttime crowd.

n somewhere in this crowd of up-ised smartphone cameras, trying move the conversation forward.

The spot where Michael Brown's body lay in the street, on the day of the shooting, before the impromptu shrine sprang up.

Every day featured multiple marches and events. Here, organizers including Anthony Shahid (in police hat) and Zaki Baruti (to his left) lead marchers past the Ferguson police station.

Protesters planted themselves in the street at dusk, usually a time of transition from the relatively peaceful daytime protests and the destruction and rioting that nighttime often brought.

he quiet before the storm. In a ghtly ritual, officers gathered in ont of the public-safety complex as otesters took to the streets.

otesters filling the street in front of e police station. The protest lead- s let it be known that their intent as to enter and occupy our head- ɪarters.

The media set up camp outside the police building.

The protesters were always clear about why they were there. They demanded an indictment of Darren Wilson; nothing less would do.

The appearance of the annual holiday decorations demonstrated the residents' determination to maintain some sense of normalcy after the city was overrun by protests and National Guard soldiers.

Preparing for the grand jury decision, the media assemble outside the county courthouse as police form a defensive line, wearing the protective gear that critics would describe as aggressive and intimidating.

The Beauty World shop, before and after: boarded up in anticipation of the grand jury decision, then in the wake of the "night of destruction" that followed the announcement.

enes of destruction,
e morning after the
nouncement of the
and jury decision, in-
ıding the QuikTrip,
w burned for the
cond time, having
eady been torched
ring the first week of
otests.

The irony speaks for itself.

Ferguson became a symbol of rage.

new firehouse next to the Ferguson police station. Here people could gather during downtimes and decompress for a few moments while enjoying great food and sharing their experiences, good and bad.

Everyone was welcome, not just the officers from the Ferguson PD. The association fed officers from neighboring municipalities, county police, state police, and even the National Guard soldiers when they were on the scene. The command posts also provided a gathering place for the many good-hearted people who came to provide aid and comfort to the weary folks of law enforcement. One afternoon as I pulled onto the PD parking lot, I was approached by an officer named Kevin Ahlbrand who wanted to introduce me to a couple of Philadelphia cops who were in town with the Billy Graham Rapid Response Team, a group of ministers and counselors, many of whom were police officers or somehow affiliated with law enforcement. One of the Philly officer volunteers was a sergeant named Kevin Bernard. Kevin explained who they were and why they were there. As people who were "on the job," they could more readily attend to the spiritual and emotional issues facing the cops who were dealing with the riots and abuse on a daily basis. I let him know that indeed, we had some officers who were having a hard time with the constant violence and hatred, and with the effect it was having on their families. Kevin made it clear that this was exactly why they had come to Ferguson. I took them inside and introduced them to Shannon, who had taken on the role of everyone's mom. She had her finger on the pulse of the department and knew who was having trouble. I felt better having these guys there. Although I had mandated everyone talk to a counselor, most officers insisted they were just fine and were reluctant to open up.

As it turned out, the experience deepened the spirit of cooperation between the various agencies on hand. Sadly, many of the African American officers were torn by conflicting loyalties. It could not have been easy for those cops to come to work every day and have to represent what some of their friends and neighbors considered to be the forces of evil.

The public conversation about policing has taken many strange twists and turns since the events in Ferguson. Dedicated professionals have faced accusations of rampant brutality, institutional racism, corruption, and basic disregard for decency or the law. However, the charge that is most relevant to the police experience in Ferguson in 2014 is the overmilitarization of the police. It's an extremely important discussion about a valid concern, but one that has been corrupted by misinformation.

When I first trained to become a police officer, it was stated openly that a police department is, for all intents and purposes, a paramilitary force. Officers are trained in weapons and tactics as well as the use of surveillance and other equipment. They are issued armored vests, helmets, and other protective gear as necessary. There is a military-style "chain of command" with a hierarchy of rank—sergeants, lieutenants, captains, and so on. We trained as a unit, the same way soldiers train as a squad or platoon. It looks and sounds a lot like the army, no doubt about it. At the same time, though, it's nothing at all like the army. The only thing police have in common with the regular military is that both groups exist to serve and protect the civilian population.

Cops do not think in terms of "the enemy." We don't train for battle. We do not automatically return fire with fire. I recall so many moments during the worst of the confrontations on the streets of Ferguson when I had the specific thought that this was not combat. In fact, our goal at all times was to avoid engagement with protesters, to avoid escalation. Time after time, police would form up in what military tacticians call a "skirmish line." The press and public would describe it in all sorts of dramatic language right out of a war novel, but in almost every case, these were lines of defense, a mobile barrier between a crowd intent on vandalism or destruction and residents' homes and property. Yes, sometimes those lines were asked to advance on a crowd to clear a roadway or to de-escalate tensions, but they did so always without injury to any citizen. If any of these actions had been military actions, the police would have protected themselves from the rocks, bottles, firebombs, and gunfire by going on the offensive and neutralizing the "enemy." That never happened.

Other specific tactics and equipment sparked outrage. After the first couple of nights in which the protests turned into riots, the commanders ordered the cops to dress in riot gear—vests, helmets, face masks, and so on. It would have been grossly irresponsible not to protect our officers in the face of a constant barrage of death threats and assaults. Anyone who followed the troubles in Ferguson knows how the press portrayed this simple sensible decision as police aggression. The idea was that police wore riot gear to the scene of a demonstration as an intimidating show of force. To this day, I am amazed that people could believe that some chief or captain thought, "We'll show up in battle dress and scare the hell out of them." Our actions were purely defensive, not offensive.

At one point, cops were even instructed not to wear protective gear, as if that would de-escalate the tension. Of course, all it did was put cops unnecessarily at risk. The same thing happened with tear gas, on several occasions, one involving a high-ranking Justice Department official who insisted that such tactics made for terrible optics. No commander believed for even a second that optics were more important than the safety of their officers. I discussed this in detail in chapter 3, but the basic point is that no one has yet come up with a safer, more effective tool for dispersing a mob than tear gas. Tear gas is awful. It causes significant pain to the eyes, throat, and lungs, but that pain is short-lived. Everybody recovers. I'd be delighted if someone could point me to another means of dispersing a violent crowd that doesn't involve either a physical confrontation or a weapon that could cause more serious permanent damage.

The job of the police in Ferguson was to protect the citizens, their property, and the infrastructure of the community. The alternative to clearing out the rioters was to sit back and watch stores and homes get looted and burned, cars destroyed in the street, public buildings attacked, and people hurt. That was not an option. Destruction of lives and livelihoods in Ferguson would never bring back Michael Brown. It could never achieve any kind of "justice."

I've described the many different kinds of training police receive these days. Beyond the tactical training, they have to learn about mental illness, family counseling, cultural awareness, conflict resolution, and so on. One of the main focuses of training in today's world has to do with acts of terrorism. How often and in how many cities over the last ten years have police been called to respond to active-shooter situations? It doesn't matter to the police if it's political terrorists from overseas or some crazed teenager with an automatic rifle. We have to be prepared to protect any and all public spaces: schools, movie theaters, churches, shopping malls, night clubs, and so on. My department put in countless hours of training, so we'd know how to evacuate people in the fastest, safest way, although the only surplus vehicle Ferguson had was a Hummer, painted like a Mayberry black-and-white patrol car with a D.A.R.E. bear decal on the side. The larger departments in the area were lucky enough to have acquired armor-plated vehicles—people movers—with which we could move large numbers of officers into a danger zone quickly and safely, and also get citizens out of harm's way just as quickly and just as safely.

On the night the grand jury decision was announced, for instance, all the information we had told us to prepare for intense, violent, and destructive rioting, probably the worst we had yet witnessed, regardless of the actual verdict. Intelligence analysts, using a complex set of metrics and data points, estimated that there would likely be between twenty-one and twenty-seven fatalities on our streets that night. Conventional patrol cars, police vans, or even standard buses would never have kept citizens safe, nor allowed us to transport officers efficiently, under those circumstances.

Those people movers are the "military vehicles," the "tanks," that so outraged observers during the Ferguson riots. Tanks have weapons. They have cannons and machine guns and firing ports. So do most military vehicles, which are designed for combat. At no time was any such vehicle used in Ferguson. Those vehicles did often have an officer on top with a rifle, which was standard procedure for the active-shooter situations for which the police train. In retrospect, it's easy to see how that single armed officer could easily have created an aggressive and intimidating image, but unfortunately, nobody in command recognized that until it was too late.

The bottom line is that what everybody condemned as military-like and "storm trooper" tactics were never anything of the kind. I'm sure that some bad decisions were made, and that police could have handled many situations better. But in my mind, I keep returning to the simple fact that throughout all those long nights of trouble, nobody was seriously injured. I've been raked over the coals for saying as much. I've been asked, "Are we supposed to be happy just because you guys didn't hurt anybody?" My answer is that I'm happy, and very proud, about that. The Ferguson police officers, and all the other law enforcement people on the scene were attacked night after night for months. They never forgot their duty, never let their frustration get the better of them, never retaliated, never once lost faith.

The changing of the guard to a kinder, gentler police presence was a disaster. There was an enormous amount of pressure on the police to "stand down," to resist employing any equipment and tactics that could be interpreted as aggressive or hostile. When the police were ordered to back off, citizens took it upon themselves to fill the breach, to place themselves between the protesters and shops and businesses that kept Ferguson going. It was more than the cops on hand could tolerate. We are called to this work.

One officer from another force who had been assigned to help out in Ferguson summed it up. He was a military man and had served in Afghanistan, but nothing had ever made him feel as bad as when he had to follow the order to stand down in the face of rioting in Ferguson. He said he saw that order not to act, to be told to "let them vent" and be a witness to rioting, rather than to do something that could increase public safety, as an outright violation of the oath he had taken as a police officer.

Chapter 6

Politicians Fiddle while Ferguson Burns

I've been around politicians my entire adult life. I've worked hand-in-hand with local mayors and city managers and councilmen and women, state governors and attorneys general, US senators, and other federal officials. I wouldn't want to make blanket general statements about politicians, any more than I'd want people to do that about cops or protesters or any group of people. There are some rotten apples, and certainly some who always seemed more interested in the game of politics than in the work of government, but most of the politicians I've observed on the job seem as serious about their responsibilities as any other professionals I've worked with. I will say this, though: they all tend to want to keep their jobs, which means it is very important for them to look good to their constituents.

During the troubles in Ferguson in the summer and fall of 2014, a number of the politicians to whom I felt close absolutely rose to the occasion, doing their level best to support any effort to relieve tensions, restore order and civility, and protect our community for the future. The key players in the Ferguson city government—the city manager, John Shaw, and mayor, Jim Knowles—gave the maximum effort, for which the only reward they received was being slapped down hard by the Department of Justice report. Despite the DOJ's scathing and biased descriptions, these two men were part of the fabric of Ferguson, popular and respected throughout the different parts of the community, not that it saved them in the end.

Mostly, the politicians in Missouri were unable to provide genuine leadership. They could not find the right balance between effective action and good public relations. To be fair, nobody could. We tend to forget that electing people to high office doesn't suddenly grant them superhuman wisdom. They're people like the rest of us, and we have to remember that we were all facing an unprecedented, irrational, and prolonged situation in Ferguson.

On the state level, two key officials—the governor and the state attorney general—consistently proved that they weren't quite up to the challenges in Ferguson. Jay Nixon, the second-term Democratic governor—mind you, a Democrat from rural Missouri could easily be mistaken for a moderate Republican in the Northeast or on the West Coast—had retained a pretty high level of popularity throughout his productive tenure in office. He would soon be leaving, thanks to term limits, but was thought to be a rising star on the national scene. At the time, Missouri insiders whispered about his being a potential running mate for Hillary Clinton two years down the road. Nixon was ambitious enough to suit those rumors, but although he was a true Missourian, the governor had a reputation for being a little aloof, inaccessible to the state legislature. He was known to work mostly through staff and surrogates. I had occasion to meet with him in a professional capacity in the past, but I doubt he would have remembered any personal connection, given the thousands of people the governor must meet.

The series of meetings that we began to hold right after the trouble started in Ferguson perhaps jogged his memory. A couple of days after the shooting, when the protests had become nonstop, and the violence flared up many times each day, the political and law enforcement leadership gathered at the St. Louis County Police headquarters to coordinate our plans to maintain safety in the area. Governor Nixon was a key player in these meetings, which were also attended by Chris Koster, the state attorney general, and their local counterparts, Jim Knowles, John Shaw, and Bob McCulloch, the St. Louis County prosecutor. Jon Belmar, Colonel Ron Replogle, the superintendent of the Missouri State Highway Patrol, and several others represented law enforcement, later including Captain Ron Johnson. The group also maintained a liaison with the FBI, the only federal agency involved at that point. Their resources helped the rest of the team plan for what might be coming down the road.

From the start, Jay Nixon seemed primarily focused on the optics of the political response. The team's priority was to stop the spread of violence in the streets, and with luck, eliminate it completely. The hope was that this could be accomplished with a minimum of arrests, and without endangering any of the citizen protesters. A local police force like Ferguson's could handle crowd control, but we had nothing in our toolkit to handle long-term rioting on the scale we were witnessing. Even the St. Louis County police felt overwhelmed. The chiefs and commanders present all felt that the National Guard, which trains specifically for this level of civil disobedience, would be invaluable in controlling the chaos in Ferguson. Deploying the Guard would also stream-line the command structure for law enforcement, which, for the time being, involved coordinating numerous agencies and police forces.

Nixon was having none of it, though, stating straight out that we would not be deploying the National Guard. "We are going to handle this in blue," he declared, meaning that the responsibility for keeping the peace in Ferguson would fall entirely on the shoulders of the outmanned police.

"We don't want this to be another Kent State," Nixon added. On the one hand, one could argue that this first prior-ity was to protect innocent lives, if the National Guard were to start shooting. On the other hand, this comment seemed to imply that our governor didn't trust the National Guard to do its job properly, as if these troops, deployed at his dis-cretion, would suddenly get randomly trigger-happy. Nixon's comment also hinted at his concern for optics; the last thing he wanted, particularly at that moment in his political career, was to be the guy who sent federal troops in to quell what the media insisted on describing as "peaceful" protests.

To the law enforcement professionals involved, his deci-sion seemed short-sighted at best. Why would we decide against using the best available resources to maintain pub-lic safety, and risk prolonging the rioting even further? We understood that we were all in uncharted waters, and lacked the experience to help bring the situation to the best resolu-tion. For better or for worse, Jay Nixon proceeded with total faith in the local and state police, relying on the established "Code 1000," the assemblage of personnel from all the sur-rounding agencies, to handle things.

Of course, it didn't take long for events to overtake the governor's intentions. Once Ron Johnson was put in charge of security in the West Florissant corridor, his tactics, designed to soften the police presence and reduce the tensions had in fact emboldened the protesters, increasing the violent conflict. A few days after the first meeting of this leadership, at which we were told to forget about assistance from the Guard, a decision came down from Jefferson City to deploy them, by order of Jay Nixon, at the request of the Highway Patrol. It was the right thing to do, but that does not mean that it played out well. The governor had it right about public opinion. The outcry, both on the street and in the press, began immediately. They're bringing in the army! To stifle free speech! The government is attacking us! It was all about police aggression and militarization. Nobody was able to look beyond the stock protest narrative to see that deployment of the National Guard might have been the safest, quickest way to bring an end to the violence. The public's mistaking such defensive measures for acts of aggression became an inescapable part of the story line in Ferguson for many months. In the eyes of the world, it seemed, the violence in Ferguson was all our fault.

In addition, the hope that this would ease the logjam of commanders on the scene was misplaced. Chief Belmar's people were tasked with meeting with the National Guard commanders to set strategy and tactics, but that all got sticky pretty fast. Maybe the military officers didn't take kindly to policemen telling them what to do, or maybe it was a simple old-fashioned turf war, but the addition of the Guard only added to the confusion and inconsistency of command.

As the situation on the ground got worse, our governor adopted a lower and lower profile, until he all but disappeared from public view. This at a time when the community was crying out for forceful and even-handed leadership. With the media still screaming that law enforcement had become unnecessarily provocative—the problem rather than the solution—the National Guard was quietly removed from the scene, only two or three days after they had arrived.

For a while, the only time I heard from anyone in the governor's office was when someone felt the need to turn up the pressure on me to resign. It was some time before the governor again had any relevance to the events in Ferguson, and then, it was mostly to point out his own irrelevance. In the meantime, my biggest problem in state government was the state attorney general, Chris Koster. Up until the events of 2014, I had no bad feelings toward Koster, and had no reason to think he had any problems with me.

Koster had begun his political career as a Republican state senator in Missouri, but he had broken with his party over an issue that was also important to me personally: stem cell research. In 2006, Missouri enacted an amendment to the state constitution that allowed stem cell research within the state. As the leader of the Missouri chapter of the Juvenile Diabetes Research Foundation, I was an ardent supporter of the amendment, believing that this kind of research is crucial to finding cures for many diseases. I got to know Chris Koster, as well Claire McCaskill, the Democratic nominee for the US Senate at the time, who was also instrumental in getting the bill passed. The amendment became a highly charged political issue in our state but narrowly passed. McCaskill was elected to the US Senate, and a year later, Koster officially switched parties, becoming a Democrat. I believed I could count on some kind of support from both of these politicians, especially from the attorney general, the top law enforcement official in the state, who was responsible for compiling the state's statistics on racial profiling. That belief would prove to be completely misguided.

In October, it was two months after the shooting of Michael Brown and Ferguson had been overtaken by protests and rioting. Chris Koster convened a series of meetings to devise strategies, not only for resolving the ongoing unrest, but also for healing our broken community. These meetings were attended by largely the same cast of characters who Governor Nixon had convened during the summer: local and state politicians and representatives of all the relevant law enforcement agencies, with the addition of Lacy Clay, the US congressman representing District 1, which includes St. Louis and Ferguson. Koster, who by this time was extremely anxious to see me step down from my job, did not include me in these discussions.

A number of people I knew well and trusted were at those meetings and kept me well informed about the games Chris Koster was playing. The attorney general, and most of the other higher level politicians involved, desperately needed to show the public that they could take some sort of decisive action that showed how well they listened to the desires of their constituency. It didn't matter if that action was purely symbolic, or whether it was fair or justified, or whether it would have any practical purpose. What they needed was for a head to roll, and when it became clear that nobody was going to summarily fire Darren Wilson, they turned their focus to me.

I had become the face of the supposedly oppressive white power structure in Ferguson, the highest profile villain in this drama. My department had stepped back from the investigation and from riot control, but the world still saw me as the white police chief who hadn't fired Darren Wilson. That made me the most likely scapegoat, the most valuable person who could be thrown under the bus. I had known for weeks that a lot of people inside government believed that my resignation would go a long way toward appeasing the angry protestors. I still had a job to do, though, and I wasn't going to turn my back on my town. Nobody was more determined, and more devious, about forcing me to resign than Chris Koster. If all the politicians were running scared, he was at the head of the pack. That became crystal clear in the course of these meetings.

The idea had been for every attendee to bring something to the table, some tangible practical action they could take, either to help restore order in the short term or to improve circumstances in Ferguson over the long term. Koster hoped that the group would be able to present a package to the public as a demonstration of government responsiveness. And what he expected the town of Ferguson to bring to the table was my head.

I heard through Jon Belmar that Koster continued to grow more and more agitated about my refusal to resign, but the people whose opinion actually mattered the most to me—the Ferguson mayor and city manager—never gave even the slightest hint that they believed I should resign. I think that city council members were probably scared out of their minds about what was happening in our town, and so refrained from making grand public statements on my behalf, but in private, one-on-one, I felt their complete support during the crisis, just as I had the entire time I worked in Ferguson. I got the same unwavering support from the men and women of our police department, who were imploring me to hang in there.

I strongly believe that Koster and others pressured the Ferguson leadership to fire me, which they were not actually free to do, which leads to another interesting subplot. One year earlier, the Missouri legislature had enacted a law that made it much harder to fire police chiefs for political reasons or other petty squabbles unrelated to their performance on the job. The "just cause" law, as most people called it, had been pushed by law enforcement and other groups to limit the impact of changing city administrations on the stability and continuity of police departments. Although that was not the situation with me, the law effectively shielded me.

Things came to a head in early November, as the city—and the nation—braced for the St. Louis County grand jury's decision on whether to indict Darren Wilson on criminal charges. We kept hearing that decision was imminent. The tension grew in town, and within law enforcement circles, with each new day that didn't bring an announcement. The proceedings of the grand jury remained secret, of course, but few of us believed there would be an indictment. We were all equally certain that anything less than an indictment on a murder charge would ignite a whole new level of protest and rioting. We were also informed that if there was a murder indictment, it was likely there would be celebratory rioting.

On October 28, I got a call from Jon Belmar. If anybody in town knew what I was up against, it was Jon, and I depended on him to be straight with me. Jon must have gotten wind of something, because the purpose of his call that day was to urge me to resist the pressure to step down.

That same night, there was a meeting of the Ferguson town council. The meeting felt relatively calm, with much less hostility and open confrontation than we had seen in previous council meetings. But there was still national press on hand, and at one point during the evening, a reporter from CNN took me aside. He told me that he "had it on good information" that was I preparing to resign. Someone must have leaked something, perhaps hoping that if that statement got back to me, it might become true. Anyway, I made it clear to the reporter that whatever rumor he had heard was false.

That Saturday, November 1, a drug-related shooting took place on the other side of town from Canfield, leaving two young men wounded. The incident put me back on the news, and although it had nothing at all to do with the ongoing tension across town, it became one more thing hovering in the background during a closed-door meeting that took place the following Monday. Senator McCaskill and Chris Koster got a group of people together to figure out how they could induce me to resign. These were people I had known, many of them for years, and with whom I had worked productively in the past. I was fortunate that Jon Belmar attended that meeting, and texted me as it was happening to keep me informed.

I met with Belmar the next day. The hand-wringing over my resignation was really just a sideshow, a distraction from our responsibility to keep Ferguson safe in the aftermath of the impending grand jury verdict. St. Louis County had assured us all that we'd have twenty-four hours' prior notice of any announcement, but every new day with no news made us more nervous. I needed to know how Jon was planning to deploy his force before I could finalize plans for my department.

He could also fill me in on what to expect from the other law enforcement agencies involved. Naturally, we needed to know about the National Guard. Jay Nixon had mishandled the deployment of the Guard once already and was understandably gun-shy. To be fair, his use of troops had always sparked controversy, and would continue to do so. He took criticism for sending them in too hastily, but also for taking them out. Deploying those troops demonstrated his active engagement with the crisis, and his concern for the citizens and property of Ferguson. At the same time, though, federal troops—just like the use of police dogs—made for terrible optics. Nonetheless, at this point in the planning, Chief Belmar was able to state confidently that we would have access to all the National Guard members we needed.

Threats to the Ferguson police had appeared all over social media, and the mobs in the city had been chanting for a violent response if the grand jury failed to indict. Various sources throughout the city confirmed that we would be targeted. I could count on the Guard to protect our fire station and police headquarters if attacked by rioters, and to establish a strong presence along West Florissant Avenue, and even at City Hall. In fact, Governor Nixon had made a public commitment to that effect.

The grand jury kept pushing back its announcement, but we continued to prepare. On November 6, a cadre of high-ranking officers got together in the office of Richard Callahan, the United States attorney in St. Louis and top-ranking federal law enforcement official in the Eastern District of Missouri. I was in a room with Jon Belmar, Sam Dotson, commissioner of the Metropolitan Police Department in St. Louis, Ron Replogle of the Missouri State Highway Patrol, along with Captain Ron Johnson and his boss, Major J. Bret Johnson. Up until this point, our state politicians hadn't needed any help sabotaging the law enforcement efforts in Ferguson, but now it appeared that Washington wanted in on that action. It had been rumored that Eric Holder, US attorney general, would attend this meeting via conference call, but that didn't happen. Ron Davis, director of the DOJ Office of Community Oriented Policing Services, ran this particular show.

Davis had spent nearly thirty years as an officer and chief in California, and he worked with the DOJ on police reform and in its civil rights division. We all had good reason to expect him to bring a clear-eyed, no-nonsense approach to the task of ensuring safety in our community. Davis, however, had a different agenda, and it all had to do with optics. He started out by requesting that the officers at the scene make sure to tone down the police response to civil unrest. No tear gas, he said. No use of what he referred to as "military vehicles." No incitement, as if he had bought into the notion that police taking measures to protect themselves was the cause of public violence. He made it clear that the local commanders were to "control the optics."

The response among the seasoned cops in the room ranged from frustrated to outraged. Police commanders follow a strict protocol when it comes to crowd control or riots. The principle mirrors the "use-of-force continuum" that governs one-on-one encounters between an officer and a citizen. An officer begins with the least combative tactic—the mere presence of the badge and uniform—and moves to verbalization, empty-hand control, nonlethal tactics, and finally to lethal force as a last result. The same idea applies to crowds: start by hoping a police presence will keep the situation calm, then try communication, then other levels of confrontation and containment. Police don't deploy weapons or tactics before determining that previous tactics have failed and that a threat persists. During the Ferguson protests, law enforcement would establish guidelines ahead of any major event, with the goal of securing public safety while not infringing on protesters' rights, including what protest activities would or would not be acceptable, and where and when they would be acceptable. Where would we allow streets to be blocked, and for how long? Where could we establish "free speech zones?" We did everything we could to communicate all those decisions to protest leaders ahead of time. And we consciously decided to keep large armored vehicles or any other equipment that could be perceived as "tactical" out of the crowd's sight unless and until it was absolutely necessary.

Davis was asking us to prioritize public safety and officer safety behind the way things look, rather than the way things are. There wasn't a single chief present who would agree to jeopardize his people, or risk escalating riots, just to create the soothing image of kinder and gentler police.

I spoke up, telling Davis, "Your focus is in the wrong place." I pointed out the success of our tactics and practices in the ongoing unrest, even including the use of tear gas. Nobody—not one citizen or protester, and not one police officer—had been hurt throughout the previous three months of rioting, looting, setting fires, blocking traffic and transportation, and regular gunfire aimed at officers, their vehicles, and their buildings.

Davis didn't like that. "You can't tell people who have been oppressed for three hundred years that they should be glad we didn't kill them."

That is, of course, a true statement. It's a valid and important point that, to me, completely missed the point, which is what I said to Davis: "I think it's a good message that we've been taking fire, attacked with bottles of urine, fire bombs, and rocks and whatever, and instead of retaliating, we've kept people from getting hurt." He didn't care that it had felt like we had been under siege for months.

The Missouri officers walked out of that meeting shaking their heads. Belmar, for one, said he'd absolutely use tear gas if he thought it was the safest way to control crowd violence. Davis, representing the DOJ, had wasted our time with ridiculous requests, and had squandered a real opportunity. What became clear to me was that the administration, as far as it was going to be involved in the Ferguson situation, had its own agenda and its own priorities. Washington needed to be seen as taking an active role in healing communities, easing racial tensions, in seeing that justice was done, whatever that had come to mean in this case.

Listening to the condescending Davis was hugely frustrating. My colleagues and I were pissed that he talked to us as if we weren't after exactly the same things as the administration, and always had been. But I wasn't about to let people start attacking each other in the streets of Ferguson; I wasn't about to watch my town go up in flames; and I wasn't about to needlessly put my guys' lives at risk so that politicians could look good.

There was more bad news. As we walked out to our cars, Jon Belmar took me aside.

"Hey, I gotta tell you something." Clearly Jon wasn't happy about what he had to say. "I know I told you that the National Guard would be coming into Ferguson. It's not." Jon pointed at an abandoned building down the block. "The National Guard will stand in front of that building before they'll show up in Ferguson."

I asked him if he knew why. "Is this because I'm not resigning?"

"I don't know," Belmar answered. "I wish I could tell you." He couldn't even tell me who had been responsible for that decision, only that one of his top officers had heard it from a colonel in the Guard with whom he had been coordinating. I asked if the federal soldiers would at least be present inside of buildings so I could bring my officers out into the street, and he told me no, the National Guard would be nowhere in Ferguson.

The very next day, I got the call on my cell phone from Senator Claire McCaskill, which I've previously mentioned. "You haven't done anything wrong," she said, "but we need to start over, with a clean slate. It's not fair, but it's necessary." Immediately after the call, the senator repeated her call for my resignation, only this time, she did it publicly, on local news radio. It would be a stretch to say that McCaskill had been a friend, but we certainly were not strangers. I had worked with the senator in support of important stem-cell research initiatives that had been critical to the success of her last campaign, and which had also figured prominently in Chris Koster's political career. Regardless of whatever mutual respect might have existed between us, she believed that if someone from within the perceived power structure fell on their sword, it would help quiet the unrest. And she wanted that someone to be me.

The issue continued to heat up. Belmar got me on the phone that same evening to say that Chris Koster had told him he had heard I was resigning the next day. Where he would have heard that is anybody's guess. I had been meeting with my superiors, carefully weighing the pros and cons of resigning, but I can't imagine that's where Koster's information came from. I asked Jon to let Koster know that I wasn't going anywhere. When Jon called back a little while later, he told me that the attorney general "went nuts."

Chris Koster's meetings about the future of Ferguson were proceeding, and he wanted me to know that "he had people coming in from out of town" to announce all the good things they were going to do if I quit. The implicit message is that now I was standing in the way of those good things, although he never made clear what they were. There had certainly been plenty of meetings to which I hadn't been invited, and perhaps various promises had been made in those sessions. Koster called a press conference for a couple of days later, at which he would announce this sudden interest in, and influx of resources to, Ferguson. I think he assumed he'd also be announcing my resignation at the same conference.

Again, Jon Belmar urged me to stand firm, but still, I agonized about the decision put before me. I absolutely wanted what was best for Ferguson and wouldn't have hesitated to step down if I knew it could help. At the same time, I had a lot of other factors to consider, well beyond my personal stake in what was, after all, my community, too. My bosses and I knew that the Ferguson police force would be devastated if they saw their chief turn his back on the situation. How could we demoralize these officers even further, as they braced themselves for still more turmoil in the streets? Did it really make sense to sacrifice the relationships I had built with so many people, not just within the various groups of protesters but throughout the city and with every branch of government and law enforcement? I still had a department to run—a full time job even without the daily rioting—and I couldn't imagine turning it over to a newcomer, especially in the middle of such a mess. Who would that benefit? Besides, who would have wanted the job?

That all added up to a significant counterweight to the optics of my stepping down. Besides, I suspected that all those people who wanted me gone were overestimating the benefit of the optics. For sure, I had become one of the prominent lightning rods, but at the same time, there was more than enough hostility to go around. I knew better than to believe that the storm would blow over just because there was one less white police chief. Anyway, from what I was hearing, a lot of promises made behind closed doors were already in the process of unraveling.

It was turning out to be a hell of a week. On November 10, I appeared before the grand jury, which of course meant facing a fleet of press trucks outside the courtroom, each with a reporter asking questions I couldn't answer. My experience in front of the grand jury confirmed my sense that there would be no indictment of Darren Wilson. I remember one questioner asking me if I thought it was common knowledge that Ferguson police officers didn't carry Tasers. I couldn't believe the lack of perspective, and wanted to say, "Are you kidding? A couple of months ago, it wasn't even common knowledge that there was a Ferguson, no less what kind of equipment the cops carry there."

After another city council meeting later that night, my phone rang again. This time, it was Tony Vermillion, the head of security for Emerson Electric, wondering if I'd meet him for coffee in the morning. This was a man I knew well enough, given the prominence of Emerson in our community, and the many times I'd needed to coordinate with him, but I sensed something unusual about his invitation. A reporter I knew clued me into the fact that the meeting the next morning was actually at the request of the state attorney general, Chris Koster.

Vermillion dispensed with the small talk pretty quickly when we met for coffee the next day. "I'm just the messenger," he began. He explained that Koster had asked Emerson's chief counsel to ask him to approach me about stepping down, which I already knew. Koster had wanted Tony to lean on the fact that I was only six months from retirement anyway, which in fact wasn't true. Tony didn't have a horse in this race, and he had done the favor he was asked to do, although it accomplished nothing.

Koster really seemed obsessed with getting me out. He must have told an awful lot of people that I was leaving, and now had to do anything he could to see that it actually happened. The next call I received came from Sheldon Lineback, the head of the Missouri Police Chiefs Association and the primary sponsor of the "just cause" law that protected police chiefs in the state, livid that Koster had called him asking if there was any way around the statute. Koster also called Chris Hesse, the lawyer who had drafted the law, with the same question. It's hard to know what Chris Koster was thinking at the time. How could he not know that these men had long-standing relationships with me? That they would be outraged by his desire to work around a law in which they believed deeply? Did he think they wouldn't notice that the attorney general was asking them to help circumvent one of the laws of his own state?

The attorney general finally got the message that I had no intention of resigning, and here's what happened next: he cancelled the press conference he had called. All that great stuff for Ferguson that people were coming in from Washington to announce? Up in smoke. I'll never know for certain whether my resignation was the bargaining chip that had made any of that possible, and that is of course something to come to terms with. All I know is that I wasn't the one making the important decisions in that scenario. In a footnote to that story, Chris Koster, the man who was making those decisions, lost his bid for the governorship of Missouri in the fall of 2016.

For the next couple of weeks, the politicians pretty much left me alone and let me do my job. That was a good thing, because those were two weeks of nonstop protests. The entire city of Ferguson was on pins and needles, waiting for an announcement from the grand jury. In city council meetings, on social media, and on the streets, protest leaders had threatened to "burn it down" and "kill cops" if there was no indictment. The anticipation had begun to bring more and more protesters and agitators from all over the country into Ferguson. The regular outbursts of nighttime violence were starting to appear during the daytime as well. The city was on edge.

On Monday, November 24, I received notice of a press conference, to be held just two hours later, to announce another press conference later that night, at which the grand jury's decision would be made public. There was no indication of what would be announced, but I had very little doubt about what was to come. In the afternoon, the prosecuting attorney, Bob McCulloch, announced a press conference for 8 o'clock that evening. The timing sparked considerable controversy. Everybody knew that nighttime generally meant violent rioting, so that now the jury decision would come out at the most dangerous time. On the other hand, many officials expected violence regardless of the time of day, and believed it was better to let it come at night, when kids were not in school, when parents were home from work, when the streets were less trafficked. Both arguments rang true, but I expected the worst either way.

I remember standing by the window of the Ferguson police station, overlooking the street below, during McCulloch's televised press conference that night. As the prosecutor droned on with a detailed account of the grand jury's processes and procedures, I could literally watch the trouble coming, like watching a storm bear down on you from across the fields. The crowd grew steadily, and became louder, more agitated, and more threatening every minute. We had many police officers on hand, but no National Guard.

Eventually, McCulloch stated that there would be no charges against Darren Wilson, and the crowd erupted immediately. First, the phone store across from the police station was looted. Next, the crowd torched a police car parked on the street, but not before stealing the AR-15 assault rifle from within it. It wasn't long before we heard the distinctive sound of the shots from that weapon amid the gunfire already filling the air. Store windows were smashed and the looting began; people were yelling and running in every direction.

At first, I went out to the rear of the police station, where rioters were gathering force. Shots were coming from the crowd, aimed at officers and vehicles and generally at the building itself. The police took cover but stayed calm, withstanding but never returning the gunfire. We did deploy tear gas, which in combination with our refusal to escalate the situation, soon dispersed the crowd, who appeared to abandon the attempt to occupy the stationhouse.

I ventured further out to meet the arriving SWAT truck, and saw that the police station was now surrounded by thousands of people, tearing down whatever they could, setting fire to whatever would burn, shooting guns in the air, at the stationhouse, and now it seems, at the police on the street. I remember at one point a firetruck rolling in to deal with the multiple fires now burning, and a group of rioters literally trying to carjack it. People suddenly swarmed all over the truck, while others fired their guns at the terrified firemen on board. Some told me later they were sure they would die on that truck. I'm still amazed that none did.

The SWAT captain, my old friend Kurt Frisz, made the decision to deploy tear gas in the hopes of dispersing the dense crowd of armed rioters. The gas actually worked, and the rioters splintered off into smaller groups around town. As the rioters spread out, so did the destruction. Something like sixty different Ferguson businesses were vandalized that night. Some were completely destroyed. It almost felt like there was a kind of twisted system to the attacks. Someone would set a fire. A crowd would gather and wait for the firetrucks and other emergency vehicles to arrive. Then they would start shooting at the firefighters and rescue personnel, keeping them all trapped inside their trucks. They'd wait like that, holding everyone at bay until the fire was burning out of control, engulfing the entire building, and only then move on to find something else to torch. Set fire, open fire, wait, repeat. It was absolutely one of the most surreal and night-marish nights of my life as a policeman.

My assistant chief, Al Eickhoff, and I circulated around city trying to help control various pockets of violence and looters, as did Jon Belmar. It was, in a word, overwhelming—even with hundreds of police officers, there was nothing we could do to stop the violence—and we began literally begging for assistance from the National Guard. The city manager and the mayor of Ferguson were calling everyone they could think of at every level of state government, asking about the Guard, but they got nowhere.

What was so frustrating was that the Guard was deployed in the city of St. Louis, and in the county seat of Clayton, where they had nothing to do. Moreover, we'd come to know these troops, and felt sure that they very much wanted to come to Ferguson and help keep the peace. So much destruction could have been prevented. I'll never know if this was about optics, about retaliating for my refusal to resign, or about something else entirely. All I know is that whoever decided to hold the National Guard out of the fray that night did a terrible disservice to the people of Ferguson.

About 2 o'clock in the morning, a busload of National Guard soldiers showed up in front of the police station. The troops got out, lined up, and paraded around for a minute or two, then got back on their bus and left. I guess now it could at least be said that they were there. Another squad marched down West Florissant Avenue, but by that time, twenty-six buildings were on fire, vehicles were burning, and shops were destroyed all over town. The community, my community, was ravaged by the flames of burning rage.

The entire episode would come back to haunt Governor Jay Nixon, who up until that summer had ambitions for national office. Neither the press nor the public minced any words regarding his indecisive and uncertain leadership during the unrest, especially in the weeks leading up to the grand jury announcement. In a conference call with the press in late November, a reporter posed a simple question.

"Does the buck ultimately stop with you?"

Nixon's response, captured on tape and replayed virally on the internet, said nothing, but also, pretty much said it all.

> We're, um, you know, it uh, it uh, you know, our goal here is to, is to, you know, keep the peace and allow folks' voices to, uh, uh, to be heard. Um, and in that balance, I'm attempting, you know I am, using the resources we have to marshal to be predictable, uh, for both those pillars. I, I don't, I'm more . . . I, I have to say I don't spend a tremendous amount of time personalizing this vis-a-vis me.

At this point I think it's fair to remind readers that the question to the governor was "does the buck stop with you?" He continued:

> I'm trying to make sure that, uh, um, that, that we move forward in a predictable, peaceful manner that plans for all contingencies that might occur so that people of a disparate group of opinions and actions can, can be heard while at the same time the property and, and persons, personal, persons of people in the St. Louis region are protected. So, that, I mean, uh, I'd, I'd prefer not to be a commentator on it.

As Kevin McDermott of the *St. Louis Post-Dispatch* observed, "Harry Truman, it wasn't."

The narrow-minded perspective that Ron Davis of the DOJ had brought with him proved to be fairly typical of Washington's view of the events in Ferguson. Like everybody else, Attorney General Eric Holder, and to a lesser extent, even President Obama, seemed to accept the media narrative without question. Police and law enforcement had acted wrongly, or hastily, or irresponsibly in the initial shooting, had compounded that error by overreacting to the protests, and all of that happened in the context of a local criminal justice system that was designed to discriminate. In fact, just a couple of weeks before Michael Brown's death, Obama had orchestrated his "beer garden summit," where he invited the academic and activist Henry Louis Gates Jr. to have a beer at the White House with the police sergeant who had handcuffed and detained him in an incident that received national attention. It was admirable of the president to do what he could to focus the public's attention on issues like racial profiling, but he unwittingly helped set the tone, making people more likely to jump to conclusions about police wrongdoing.

In his first public comments after the shooting, Obama tried hard to be fair and to withhold judgment. He condemned the protesters for attacking police and for destroying property, but also stated that excessive force from law enforcement in order to stifle peaceful protest was unacceptable. The president wanted to be a calming voice in the chaos, but it was a pretty easy thing to say from his Martha's Vineyard vacation. No law enforcement people on the ground in Ferguson disagreed, but we had not seen any examples of excessive force as we tried to maintain order while allowing protests to continue round the clock. Obama went on to talk about communities without hope, about young men without jobs or schooling—all crucially important issues underlying tensions with police in many cities. I fear that well-intentioned comments like this just reinforced that narrative that Michael Brown's death was somehow attributable to racial inequality under the law, rather than about an officer fending off repeated attacks from an individual.

When President Obama announced that he was sending Attorney General Eric Holder to Ferguson to oversee the investigation, we felt a shift in the agenda. He made his presence more about his cultural identity than about his position as the top law enforcement person in the country, stating that he might be the attorney general, but he was "also a black man." Holder made it clear from the start that this was to be an investigation into the possible violation of Michael Brown's civil rights, all but saying outright that it had been a bad shooting. At no time did he make any public statement that indicated the Justice Department might be wanting to protect the reputation of an officer who had fired his weapon in self-defense. Jay Nixon had done much the same thing when he stated that there would be a "vigorous *prosecution*" into the shooting rather than simply a vigorous investigation.

The attorney general came to Ferguson, where he met with Michael Brown's family and spoke not about seeking impartial justice, but about justice "for Michael Brown." He embraced Ron Johnson, the highway patrol captain, but never came to meet with any of the other law enforcement commanders, all of whom, in theory at least, work for him. Even when the grand jury declined to indict Darren Wilson, Holder "reassured" the crowds that it wasn't necessarily the final say in the matter because the DOJ investigation was independent and still in progress. The federal investigation completely backed up the grand jury's findings in the end.

To me, an early indicator of bias against law enforcement was when the White House announced its decision to send three staff members to Michael Brown's funeral. I do not wish to downplay the family's heartbreak, or to imply that it's incorrect to pay respect, but such decisions have to be taken in context. There were funerals of military personnel killed in combat as well as national and international leaders to which the White House sent fewer representatives, or in some cases, none at all. At no time did anyone from the White House, or from the attorney general's office, contact the police commanders who were risking their lives twenty-four hours a day for weeks and months on end, to offer support or encouragement, or even simple words of understanding.

Inequality, injustice, and discriminatory treatment by the justice system are real. Nobody in public service would argue the point. I don't fault the administration for seizing the opportunity to raise awareness and spark public discussion, but to do that in a way that poisoned the atmosphere around what happened in our town, to real people who had to suffer the consequences, was nothing short of shameful. Even worse, it turned out to be only the tip of the iceberg. None of us had any idea what we were in for once the Department of Justice really set its sights on Ferguson.

Chapter Seven

A Biased Report about Bias

The uproar that tore apart Ferguson had been predicated on a falsehood. Whether it began as an intentional lie or a tragic misperception, the false narrative of how Darren Wilson came to shoot Michael Brown that day became the myth that fueled the public's outrage and underlying assumption of virtually all the press coverage. For me, the final disillusionment, the last awful irony, was that the damning report on Ferguson from the United States Department of Justice, the final nail in the coffin for our community, was itself a collection of misperceptions, misrepresentations, and outright falsehoods.

This is the most painful part of the story for me, and the most difficult to discuss. I can remain calm surrounded by protesters, but I can't always set aside my anger over what I believe is an unfair condemnation. I feel like I've been wrongly convicted in some kind of show trial in a kangaroo court, stripped of my position and livelihood—a lifetime of committed service up in smoke. Every time I try to talk about the unfairness of the DOJ report, I feel like people must think I'm some kind of crackpot, like the conspiracy theorists who think that the moon landing was faked or that the 9/11 attack was some kind of inside job. Yet the report is so horrific, so over the top, I wonder how anyone could take it at face value, how anyone could believe that a town and a police department as cruel and corrupt as the one depicted in those pages could have survived in any American city for any amount of time. To me, the very idea is inconceivable and absurd.

It is my belief that the men and women of the DOJ's Civil Rights Division who researched and compiled this "pattern-or-practice" report, the *Investigation of the Ferguson Police Department*, failed in their duty to uphold basic principles of fairness and justice in order to make public a conclusion their boss had reached before even arriving in Ferguson.

From the moment Attorney General Eric Holder arrived in town, the scales of justice were heavily tipped against our police department and city management, in the court of opinion, at least. If we learned nothing else from the crisis in Ferguson, we learned that the court of public opinion is pretty much the only court that matters. The US attorney general coming to town, letting the world know he was there to meet with the "victim's family," never speaking to me or to the other law enforcement officials ostensibly under his command, right away tipped public sympathy away from the truth and in favor of the media narrative of injustice and brutality. That he then ordered a federal investigation, assigned to his department's Civil Rights Division, sent an unmistakable signal that he wanted to believe that Michael

Brown's death had resulted from some kind of violation or wrongdoing.

As if there wasn't already enough bad blood between Holder and his team and the Ferguson leadership, there was another dustup at the time of the press conference at which I released the convenience store video involving Michael Brown and Dorian Johnson. As I described earlier, we had gone to great pains to meet first with representatives of the Brown family and explain why we had to make the video public, and help them prepare for whatever fallout that might trigger. A representative from the DOJ Community Relations Service had been present at that meeting, and had let us know that the department would weigh in prior to the press conference, with recommendations on how to proceed. We never heard from them, and yet later, the DOJ scolded us publicly for not following their recommendations.

In its online reporting on Holder's visit at the time, CBS News said, "Holder's efforts so far are encouraging to those looking for reforms to the systemic problems that led to Brown's shooting on Aug. 9 and the subsequent unrest in Ferguson, such as racial inequities in the criminal justice system and mistrust between local police forces and the communities they protect. Still, they're looking for a commitment to reform from the Justice Department that will last long after the dust settles in Ferguson." Are there systemic problems that led to Michael Brown's shooting? Absolutely. Almost too many to count. Is the criminal justice system in need of deep and lasting reform? No doubt. But to this day, there is no evidence of any link between Michael Brown's death and any unfair treatment by law enforcement or the justice system, and yet they will always be linked in the minds of the American people, in part because of Eric

Holder's early statements. I assume that Mr. Holder had the best of intentions, but he came to the Ferguson situation with a bone to pick.

As previously discussed, Holder further fanned the flames of conflict by issuing a statement upon his visit, in which he talked about the need to rebuild trust between police and the public, but laid it all on the cops to stop sending a "conflicting message" by using unnecessary "military equipment and vehicles." It goes without saying how inappropriate it was for the ranking law enforcement figure in the country to be perpetuating and reinforcing this militarization narrative, especially since the source of much of the equipment was the US Department of Justice through its Bureau of Justice Assistance. I also ask myself how open and fair I would have been if I were sent to Ferguson to write a report, knowing my boss had such strong preconceptions about what would be discovered.

Holder's public stance actually worked against the interests of fairness and against the notion of justice being blind. The attorney general actually painted himself into a corner. Reporter Richard A. Serrano in the *Los Angeles Times* described Holder's investigation of Ferguson as "unusually aggressive," and cited anonymous Justice Department officials who asserted first that "the more he gets out in front publicly, the more he will be expected to deliver criminal charges," and then further, that "the situation could reach a tipping point where federal criminal charges would be the only way to vindicate Holder's public comments and show that the federal government is serious." In addition, he played to a sympathetic audience by speaking publicly about his own experiences being unfairly profiled by police when he was a young man. Eric Holder was the face of law enforcement in America, but at the same time, he had aligned himself with factions who were ready to blame police before the facts of the case had been sorted out.

I was well aware of the accepted narrative, and of how Holder's public comments and actions had reinforced that narrative, but still, I came to my early meetings with the Department of Justice hopeful that at least we had clear-eyed legal authorities from the federal government who would help set things right. My colleagues in city govern-ment shared that optimism, and our first sit-down with the DOJ lawyers, shortly after Holder's visit, went well. Our city leaders—John Shaw, James Knowles, city attorney Stephanie Karr, and I—sat down with the DOJ team, who were, at the time, more than merely cordial. They were friendly and sup-portive, and at all times made us feel that we were all working toward the same goal. The Justice lawyers went so far as to imply that they were looking forward to clearing the air and that there was nothing for any of us to worry about. The lead investigator, Christy E. Lopez, casually mentioned that after flying back to Washington, they would consider the possibil-ity of opening a "pattern-or-practice" study of Ferguson, but downplayed it, telling us that it would be no big deal.

Imagine my surprise when, literally, as I walked out of that meeting, a reporter from CNN took me aside and let me know that such an investigation had already been opened, a piece of information that had been leaked by someone in Washington. As I would later understand, Christy Lopez had built her career on investigating police wrongdoing and bringing about reform in police departments and practice. I don't have a problem with that in principle, and in fact, Lopez has received a fair amount of public support from the law enforcement community, but her assignment to this case was yet another sign of the assumptions that the Department of Justice was bringing to Ferguson. This lack of openness and honesty, from people ostensibly on the same team as I was, shocked me. Even more alarming, the people I knew who had closer ties to the Justice Department, local employees of federal agencies like the FBI, let me know that in their experience, the Department's opening of an investigation generally meant a presupposition of guilt. They were generally far more likely to commit resources to an effort when they had confidence in the outcome.

As I hope to show you, the damning report from the Department of Justice was as much a matter of optics—from its inception right through to its execution—as anything else I witnessed during the crisis in Ferguson. Eric Holder never had to come right out and say what he believed about what happened there. His very presence in town; his public statements about his own experiences with unfair treatment by police; his meeting with the Brown family while never meeting with any local law enforcement people except Captain Ron Johnson; and his insistence on an investigation by his department's Civil Rights Division, to be led by a specialist in police misconduct, made a clear statement about where he stood. If his actions could skew the entire country's perception of the shooting and its aftermath, how could it not do the same for the investigators working for him?

I suppose one could argue that Holder's actions regarding Ferguson were the result of the public pressure on him, or on the federal government, to intervene in some way, but that still ties it all directly to optics. That the report itself would be corrupted by optics was made clear to me by Lopez herself in that first meeting. In explaining to us the nature of a pattern-or-practice report, she made it clear that they didn't play by the rules you'd expect from an investigative body but more by the rules of tabloid media. She told us, without any irony, that their investigation did not have to deliver absolute proof of racial bias, but rather only had to demonstrate that there was a credible appearance of racial bias. The investigation did not need to meet the evidentiary standards of the criminal justice system. In hindsight, this should have been a red flag.

Think about that: the Department of Justice's report would not have to meet the same standards as those to which it would ultimately hold the Ferguson police. Whereas the FBI, a branch of the Department of Justice, had been meticulous and exhaustive during its investigation of the actual shooting, the attorneys doing the pattern-or-practice study relied on anonymous or unverified/uncorroborated sources; they felt free to quote written and oral testimony out of context, to ignore exculpatory evidence and worse. However, I was not aware of their investigatory aversion to favorable evidence as they went forward with what turned out to be a witch hunt. One particular section of the report, titled "FPD Engages in a Pattern of First Amendment Violations," is supported almost entirely by anecdotal information provided by unidentified parties, with no attempt at verification through interviews or exhaustive records examinations. When the Justice investigators did look at arrest reports, they made their own findings and determinations concerning what rights had been violated, though no cases were even contested on civil rights grounds, nor were any such legal findings ever made. That didn't stop the DOJ from publishing its opinion that FPD systematically violated constitutional rights and employed excessive force to do so.

The DOJ went so far as to advertise locally, requesting people with grievances about the Ferguson police to step forward, and it was common knowledge in town that they were conducting street interviews along the West Florissant corridor with protesters who were overwhelmingly, if not entirely, from places other than Ferguson. Acquaintances of mine in the FBI let me know that when attorneys from the Civil Rights Division sat in on FBI interviews with alleged witnesses to the shooting, they repeatedly asked leading questions, in the vain hope of implicating Darren Wilson in a civil rights violation.

Within days of that first meeting, the DOJ attorneys headed full throttle into their investigation, demanding thousands and thousands of documents from our department and from the Ferguson municipal court. The records request posed particular challenges because of circumstances that no one could have foreseen. In the summer of 2014, the police and fire headquarters in Ferguson were undergoing renovation. For all intents and purposes, the building was under siege, with the vast majority of our records packed away in boxes and piled into rooms made less accessible by construction. Complicating things even further, I had launched an initiative to computerize those records early on in my tenure so they were in various states of conversion. Digging out all the records that the DOJ lawyers wanted to dig through turned out to be laborious and time-consuming, sucking up manpower that was desperately needed elsewhere. None of that stopped the Justice's final report from dinging the city for its shoddy record-keeping and lack of computerization.

After that first meeting, and the onerous request for documents, the Justice attorneys went about their business, mostly avoiding any direct consultation with me or others in the city administration, but making their presences known just the same. We were generally aware of whom they were interviewing, what kinds of questions they were asking, and what kinds of historical records they were seeking. It felt a little like the proverbial death by a thousand paper cuts, as if we were being slowly beaten down, even as the investigators kept dishonestly reassuring us, "There's nothing glaring here. Nothing you can't handle."

Looking back on it, it was clear that the Department of Justice attorneys were deliberately sandbagging us. At no time did any of them come to me or any of the other city officials and present their findings or theories, in order to discuss, understand, seek explanations, or consider alternative interpretations. And when any of us presented any information or evidence that presented a positive image of Ferguson, that information was stunningly absent from their final report. Take, for example, a study published in May 2014, only a few months before the shooting, by researchers at the University of Missouri–St. Louis. This study had been prepared as part of a proposal in which the city of Ferguson would annex an unincorporated area adjacent to the city. As part of the evaluation, the researchers had polled the residents of the city to determine their level of satisfaction with city government and services, and the findings were overwhelmingly supportive. Three-quarters (74 percent) of the respondents rated the city's overall services as good or excellent, while slightly more (76 percent) gave those high ratings to Ferguson's police protection. Only 4 percent of respondents rated the police as poor, a lower percentage than almost any other city service including the fire department. Bear in mind that Ferguson's African American population is well over 60 percent, so it's unlikely that these statistics were skewed along racial lines. Did these statistics appear in the Department of Justice report? They did not. Did the Justice attorneys seek out residents who had responded favorably, or in any way attempt to discover what might have made people feel so strongly positive about our department? Not that we could determine.

At the start of the investigation, Christy Lopez explained that her people didn't have to prove bias, but only make a case for the appearance of bias. When the report was completed and she presented it to us just prior to making it public, we were summoned to a meeting where we were required to surrender cell phones and recording devices. At that meeting, she made an even more chilling statement. Looking through the report, it was clear that our statistics were not the ones provided officially as compiled throughout the state of Missouri by Attorney General Chris Koster's office. We were told they had hired their own statistician to take other factors into consideration. We all listened in horror as she outlined the essential findings in the report. A stunned Stephanie Karr, our city attorney, protested, "You can't say that, it won't hold up in litigation." Lopez replied coldly, "Well, we aren't litigating, are we?"

Let's look at the some of the key details of the report itself, and compare them to the reality that those of us who actually lived and worked in Ferguson understood. The first main section heading in the report reads, "Ferguson Law Enforcement Efforts Are Focused on Generating Revenue." Leaving aside the obvious issues—its deliberately inflammatory nature that declares an opinion or interpretation—it is preposterous on the face of it, and gives one the sense that the people who compiled the report had no concept of how the world works. The first sentence of this section is, "City officials have consistently set maximizing revenue as the priority for Ferguson's law enforcement activity." It should be noted that no city official was asked any questions about how budget priorities were determined, or anything else about the budgeting process, for that matter.

Every organization, every business, every community that has expenses has to put together an operating budget. Whether it's a church or a garden club or a baseball team or the federal government, every group has to determine how much money it needs to cover its costs and how that money is going to be generated. Every year, everybody goes through some kind of budgeting process. If it's a company of some kind, the executive at the top asks each department head to figure out how much money that department expects to generate in revenues, and how much it will cost to create those revenues. A government goes through the same process, but vaguely in reverse. In a town like Ferguson, the city manager and finance director ask each department head—police chief, fire chief, heads of public works, recreation, and so on—how much they need to provide the required services, and then looks at the town's various revenue streams to figure out how to cover those costs. In business, the goal is profit, the difference between income and expenses. In government and other organizations, that difference would be used to improve or expand activities or services, or invested for the future.

The Department of Justice report makes this outrageous claim right up front:

> Ferguson's law enforcement practices are shaped by the City's focus on revenue rather than by public safety needs. . . . The City budgets for sizeable increases in municipal fines and fees each year, exhorts police and court staff to deliver those revenue increases, and closely monitors whether those increases are achieved. City officials routinely urge Chief Jackson to generate more revenue through enforcement.

So of course, the financial officers of the city came to me and asked me for my projections. It was part of the standard budgeting process that everyone goes through, but it is completely wrong to assume that asking for numbers is the same as applying pressure to generate additional income through police activity. That simply didn't happen, despite the one or two lines quoted out of context from internal city emails, or the anonymous, uncorroborated "sources" referred to in the report.

If the budget director asks me something innocuous like "Are you sure that's all you got?" it's not because he's pressuring me to come up with more; he's just trying to make his budget work. In fact, when he did ask, my practice was just to tell him to put in whatever number he wanted, while making the point that we did not run our police department to generate money. To me, the report's tone in this section reveals how out of touch the Department's investigators are with workings of the real world. They depict this effort to generate revenue as if it were the primary focus of our working day in the Ferguson city government. Budgeting was one of many responsibilities I juggled in my job, one that I dealt with a couple of times a year. Like any other manager in any other organization or company or agency anywhere, I treated it as a nuisance, one of the unavoidable chores of management that took time away from what I saw as my real job—policing the streets of Ferguson.

The report spends a lot of ink on the Justice Department's contention that we concentrated on traffic and other vehicular violations, as well as minor street infractions, as a means to line the city coffers, and that these efforts showed racial bias on the part of the Ferguson police because disproportionate numbers of African Americans received fines. The report contends that officers were encouraged to write as many citations as possible and were routinely rewarded for doing so. I wish to point out that no DOJ investigator ever asked me anything about this; if they had, I could have easily demonstrated to them how nothing could be further from the truth. At no time during my tenure did the number of tickets written by an officer play any role in evaluating that officer for promotion. To imply that it was an important metric unjustly diminishes the actual merits upon which we based promotions. Ferguson cops were rewarded for good police work and good test scores. Additionally, we considered diversity as a factor, although clearly the DOJ would never give us credit for that. The first promotions of African American officers to higher ranks in the history of the City of Ferguson all occurred since 2010, while I was chief.

For starters, it's hard to imagine something as race-neutral as traffic enforcement, especially when so much of it was the work of automated traffic cameras at stoplights and in especially sensitive areas, such as school zones. In fact, the installation of those cameras was specifically intended to free up officers to do more critically needed police work—some of it the various forms of "community policing" that the Department of Justice asks us to do—rather than spend their days writing traffic tickets. I actually paid close attention to how my officers spent their time, long before the shooting, and when I realized that a good 50 percent of all the traffic citations in Ferguson were attributable to only three or four out of more than fifty officers on the force, I let that handful of officers know that we believed there were more useful ways for them to be spending their time on duty.

Equally ironic was the help we didn't get from the Department of Justice. For years, one of the critical safety issues in Ferguson had been that one or two central traffic arteries served countywide traffic, bringing people from neighboring communities through Ferguson, to and from St. Louis, or to work in our own town, which provided employment for people from all over the surrounding areas. As you might expect, people routinely violated the speed limit on these through streets, generating a disproportionate number of traffic accidents. Responsibility for policing these roads fell within various jurisdictions—the state highway patrol, county police, municipal police forces—but even to do our share meant taking officers away from higher priority work. So what did we do? We applied to the US Department of Justice's Bureau of Justice Assistance for a grant to help fund interstate highway enforcement, work that we just didn't have the resources to handle. When Justice denied us that grant, we put a plan in place to have our officers put in hours beyond their regular shifts in order to patrol those roads. The city finance director and city manager were involved in those decisions, since they meant additional overtime pay.

Experience tells us the very presence of a police car on the side of the road causes drivers to reduce speed, in much the same way a police officer's uniform and badge can de-escalate a volatile situation on the street. That was our intent when we approved that overtime enforcement—to reduce violations and accidents and increase public safety through the added presence of police—not to stop more cars, write more tickets, and generate income for the city of Ferguson.

Now, it is true that Ferguson officers dealt with a great many vehicular violations in the poorer neighborhoods dominated by public housing, with largely African American populations. It's worth reiterating that our police department's increased presence in a neighborhood was always reactive—that is, in response to the number of calls for assistance from that area. If it later seemed to be proactive, or by design, that was a matter of distributing our meager resources to the areas that, according to the data, had needed them most. At no time did anyone sit down and calculate the number of fines we might collect if we hung out in certain neighborhoods writing tickets. However, what did happen is that the police received repeated calls from neighbors complaining about abandoned and derelict vehicles on their streets, about apartments with way more people living in them than were on the leases, generating more vehicles than there was parking for in the neighborhood, creating congestion and conflict.

If we respond to calls, and find cars with no tags, drivers with no licenses and no insurance, are we not supposed to write summonses for those infractions? Surely, "License and registration, please," is not a racially biased request, although some might argue that it puts more pressure on poor people who can't afford to keep those documents current. What would the Justice Department have our officers do? Should they have told offenders, "That's alright, you're poor and black, so you get a pass?" Was it up to the cop on the street to make up for the national shame of racism and failed public policy by looking the other way? In fact, our officers did routinely listen to explanations, give warnings when possible, and try to work with violators when possible. But it's asking a great deal of an individual police officer to decide when to enforce the law and when not to. That can't help but become a slippery slope, and would absolutely create more problems over time than it would solve.

With regard to traffic summons being issued disproportionately to African Americans, the report neglects to point out several mitigating factors. First, as I've described, Ferguson has several main artery roads that facilitate through traffic from neighboring communities to St. Louis and elsewhere. Virtually all of those surrounding towns have predominantly African American populations. In addition, it's been documented that the number of traffic violations is higher in the under-fifty age group than in older groups. In Ferguson, and in other inner suburbs of St. Louis, the majority of the African American population is between the ages of eighteen and thirty-five, while the majority of the Caucasian population falls into the over-fifty category. One can assume that this difference would be reflected in the traffic statistics.

The Justice Department went so far as to draw a false connection between changes made in the police department's shift schedule and the city's alleged need to generate more income from traffic fines. We did move to a rotation of twelve-hour shifts, about which Justice had this to say: "Law enforcement experience has shown that this schedule makes community policing more difficult—a concern that we have also heard directly from FPD officers."

The simple fact is that this scheduling reorganization was requested by the Ferguson police rank and file as part of the collective bargaining effort between the city and the Fraternal Order of Police, which cites "improving the working conditions of law enforcement officers" as part of its mission statement. The change, which took an entire year to get through our city council, radically increased the level of officer satisfaction, which in turn increased the positive impact the police could have on the community. The officers had more time at home with their families, including entire weekends, which had not previously been the case. They loved it so much that at least one officer, who had actually left Ferguson for a department that offered twelve-hour shifts, applied for reinstatement once we instituted that practice.

What makes this particular accusation dishonest is that the Justice investigators had complete access to the FOP's written demands that had been delivered to me when I was hired in Ferguson. The record makes it clear that twelve-hour shifts were their top priority. In addition, DOJ had all the documentation from my research into the pros and cons of that shift schedule. They knew full well that the shift change had nothing to do with creating more revenue.

The report quotes a handful of budget-related emails between me and the city budget director that actually have nothing to do with the schedule changes. Not only are the emails quoted only partially and out of context, but they're not even relevant. There's nothing sinister or greedy or racist about the city bean counter talking to department heads about ways to get his budget to square up. It wasn't pressure on me to generate income through fines, nor did I offer ways to do so. The move to a twelve-hour shift did help the department's finances, but not by increasing revenue from fines. It reduced both overtime and sick leave as it boosted morale on the force. To imply that we took this step for any ulterior motives is a blatant and shameful red herring.

The DOJ report offers a flood of statistics that seem to support a claim that Ferguson police and the Ferguson municipal court issued summons and arrest warrants disproportionately to the African American population, while somehow running a system that had that same population tied up in court cases for longer periods of time than anybody else. But remember that you can basically use statistics to make any point you want. If the DOJ went back ten years, and assembled all the warrants issued and came up with some massive number, they could say that there were half as many warrants out as there were people in Ferguson, without clarifying how many of those warrants were from before I took over, or more importantly, were for people who were not residents of Ferguson. The report, however, fails to offer any information that might put those statistics in a meaningful context. For example, did the investigators seek to provide data on citizen complaints and calls for assistance?

The police are obliged to respond to such calls, but did the DOJ mention that the majority of those calls in Ferguson came from areas with predominantly African American residents? Did Justice provided data on the number of no-shows for scheduled court appearances or failure to make timely payments of fines that eventually result in the issuing of bench warrants?

It's particularly galling that the report rakes Ferguson over the coals for tracking down people who are delinquent with fines or court appearances, as if we were on a mission to hunt down nonwhite or poor citizens and squeeze their last dollars out of them or throw them in jail. It's hard to imagine anyone thinking that this is how any civil servant wants to spend their time and energy. The Ferguson court and police provided the Department of Justice with all manner of documentary evidence of the city's efforts to ease the burden, by working with citizens to arrange alternative court dates for people who took the simple step of phoning in to explain a conflict, by having regular amnesty programs over the last several years, and most importantly, by working extensively for two years just prior to 2014 to establish alternative sentencing programs. We even secured grant money to help create community service alternatives to fines, working together with Dwayne James, an African American city council member involved in the Ferguson Youth Initiative (FYI), and some folks from the Queen of Peace Foundation.

It's shocking that the DOJ lawyers failed to present that information, since we had provided it all to them and I know that they were present in the Ferguson courtroom at the same time as the community services representatives were there to make arrangements for alternative sentences. During that same period, the city prosecutor, the judge, and I had expunged outstanding warrants that were more than ten years old and were about to do the same for five-year-old warrants. Although the Department of Justice had all of that information, they included none of it in the report. Justice did mention that Ferguson had "reluctantly" instituted some alternative sentencing practices. Ferguson had taken those steps long before the summer of 2014, well before we showed up on Justice's radar, and there had been nothing even remotely "reluctant" about it. It was the right thing for the community.

The report attacked leaders in Ferguson for indicating that failing to pay legitimate fines or to show up for court appearances or to reschedule might be due to a lack of personal responsibility on the part of the accused.

This kind of misrepresentation, through the selective use of statistics, characterizes the entire Department of Justice report. It would have been almost funny if it hadn't been so destructive; think about how ironic it is that the report resembles a prosecutor's brief, in that it cites only the pieces of evidence that support its argument. So, in that sense, the writers of the report acted as if they were preparing for trial. However, in every other sense, trial procedures—such as the basic rules of evidence—didn't apply. Most importantly, in a trial, both sides get to tell their stories and assemble the available evidence that supports their arguments. In this case, though, the Department of Justice knew that no defense would ever be presented, and it was free to ignore conflicting evidence. It failed to provide full, accurate, and meaningful information when that information didn't serve to bolster its case.

Take, for another example, the report's focus on citations issued for "Manner of Walking in Roadway" in Ferguson. That language refers to the practice, so prevalent in our town, of citizens standing, walking, or generally just hanging out in the middle of the street. It's absolutely true that the over-whelming majority of those tickets were written to African Americans and usually to younger males. Condemning the police for that is like condemning us because the majority of parking tickets were written to car owners. There's no other way to say it, but blocking the street was a "thing" among young black people in Ferguson, just like the "squeegee men" had been a thing in New York City some years back. Anybody who lived in town knew it. Young people in public housing would gather in the street, challenging motorists to get past, sometimes threatening drivers and even charging "tolls." Maybe it was a way for people trapped by poverty to demand some respect, to slap back at a society that had left them behind, but it was real and had risen to a level of a major ongoing problem in the community. A day did not go by when we did not get a call for assistance because of traffic problems created by it, from people who were prevented from getting to their homes or jobs, or local merchants whose businesses were suffering because of it. Residents rightly expected the police to address this issue. Sadly, it's difficult to point out a simple demonstrable fact like that without being tarred and feathered as a racist.

The cops in Ferguson got no satisfaction from acting on these complaints and clearing people off the streets. That's not what police work is supposed to be about, and nobody felt good about it. On top of that, it was a simple kind of enforcement that could only lead to increased tension, and had the potential of rising to a physical encounter. By now, every-body in America knows that the fatal encounter between Michael Brown and Darren Wilson started with the officer directing two young men to get out of the street. It wasn't a case of a cop randomly losing it on a pedestrian, but, sadly, one of many road-blocking encounters that had become all too routine in Ferguson. The Department of Justice's failure to offer a complete picture of that shows either shoddy, hasty, and careless investigation, or a deliberately lopsided—biased, one might say—presentation of information to the public.

The report casts all Ferguson police activity as taking place in a culture of pervasive racism, as evidenced by interdepartmental emails the investigator examined and interviews it carried out with citizens who felt they had a bone to pick with our department. Did Ferguson cops pass along some racist jokes to their coworkers via email? Yes, they did. The report cites a half-dozen such instances during my tenure as chief (and one from before that), although it does not cite emails that were provided to the investigators, from the Ferguson city manager and others, in which the offending parties were disciplined. The city took these offenses seriously, but you wouldn't know it from the DOJ report. In fact, the DOJ lawyers were fully aware of an investigation of an incident involving a racist joke circulated in the public works department. That action resulted in the demotion of an employee, but the DOJ declined to include that information, as they did with virtually every fact at its disposal that contradicted the chosen narrative of a racist culture in Ferguson.

Likewise, there were legitimate citizen complaints about abusive or racist language and treatment from a senior Ferguson officer. And again, the DOJ offers general statements that create the illusion of rampant problems when there were actually very few documented instances, and something like three-quarters of those involved a single officer. That cop, a veteran member of the force since well before I arrived on the scene, was indeed a rotten apple—a bad-tempered bully who routinely cut corners as he pursued his own outdated brand of street justice—and I had sought to get him out of the department from day one. Union rules and other labor regulations tied my hands for quite some time, but I was able to reassign him in a way that minimized potentially volatile encounters with the public, and eventually, he was gone, as were others who viewed him as a de facto leader. We had finished cleaning house long before the summer of 2014, a fact that the DOJ report did not acknowledge.

After hiding behind a very thin smoke screen of incomplete facts and unverifiable claims in its tearing down of the Ferguson police department, the Justice Department report moves on to condemn what it saw as the greater civic culture of racism and official corruption that existed in our town. As the DOJ banged these final nails into Ferguson's coffin, it seemed to no longer care about even the appearance of fairness. The heading of the final section reads, "Ferguson Law Enforcement Practices Erode Community Trust, Especially Among Ferguson's African American Residents, and Make Policing Less Effective, More Difficult, and Less Safe." Early in the section, Justice makes this assertion: "Our investigation showed that the disconnect and distrust between much of Ferguson's African American community and FPD is caused largely by years of the unlawful and unfair law enforcement practices by Ferguson's police department and municipal court described above." What's remarkable is that the only document anywhere that describes Ferguson's police and court practices as unlawful and unfair is this very report. In other words, Justice used its own theory to support another of its theories—kind of a circular argument.

I don't want to imply that the department I led was immaculate, that no Ferguson officer ever engaged in questionable behavior. No leader in any organization could make that claim, but I absolutely reject the notion that such behavior was anything close to routine, or even frequent, during my tenure, that ranking officers took no steps to investigate or correct, or failed in any way to take allegations seriously or to work to improve relations between police and the public. I am confident in the steps I took as chief in Ferguson to develop a more responsive and community-minded force, through increased training, oversight and review, improved working conditions, and improved circumstances for the residents of the town. Relying almost entirely on rumor, innuendo, anonymous sources, and unverifiable claims, the Department of Justice took it upon itself to be judge, jury, and executioner, publishing its own perceptions as if the conclusions it drew were judicial findings.

The closing section of Justice's report is riddled with phrases like, "We heard from African American residents . . . ," and "an African American man alleged . . ." and "officers allegedly called an African American woman [an epithet]." In most of the examples cited by the DOJ investigators, there isn't enough evidence provided that one could even refute it—not that anyone in authority was ever given the chance. The US Department of Justice was totally uninterested in the basic principle of giving someone a chance to face their accuser or present another side of a story. I wish I had the time and space to offer what I know about those episodes in the report with which I'm familiar; more often than not, the version offered by DOJ is incomplete, biased, and prejudicial.

I've been in enough courtrooms to know that if I were on the witness stand, and a lawyer were able to catch me in a series of lies or mistakes, eventually, my entire testimony would be thrown out. Yet this pattern-or-practice report from the US Department of Justice has been accepted as gospel despite being full of outrageous misinformation, half-truths, and outright falsehoods, hearsay, gossip, and rumor. The report is so biased, so one-sided, so inadequately researched and verified—indeed, so completely wrong—that it's impossible to know whether it's a function of the haste with which it was prepared or of a willful effort to present its predetermined conclusion, ignoring all evidence to the contrary. These reports often spend years in development, but the Ferguson report was thrown together in a few short months. At the same time, the record shows that the attorney general all but announced his belief that Michael Brown was wrongfully killed by a racist cop in a corrupt and racist city, and it's no surprise that the investigation he ordered came so quickly to that same conclusion.

Why else would the report state that the riots and looting and rage reflected years and years of pent-up distrust and resentment about the FPD's racially motivated and allegedly unlawful practices, even though it's well established that nine out of ten of the rioters were outsiders who may never have even heard of Ferguson before that summer? I remember one roster of arrests, numbering somewhere close to fifty individuals. As I read through, it was glaring to me that only three of them were locals. The domiciles listed included California and New York.

Those of us who faced the rioters knew exactly why they were rioting—because they screamed it in our faces every night for months. It was because they believed Darren Wilson had shot an unarmed black teenager whose hands were up in surrender. But the DOJ investigators started with the premise that Ferguson was a swamp of injustice, then sought out and published only information supporting that premise, regardless of its veracity.

The report cites examples of what the Justice Department determined—long after the fact—to be examples of excessive force and violations of Fourth Amendment rights. It is important to note that such findings can only be made

through due process, including hearings in which officers amplify and respond to questions about their written
incident reports. Those reports alone are not considered
sufficient basis for any legal finding, but Justice based every
assertion solely on officer reports and interviews with
allegedly mistreated citizens. No Ferguson police officer
was ever interviewed in an attempt to get a complete picture of any of these incidents, but the citizens' accounts
were repeated in the report virtually verbatim, with no
fact-checking.

People will say what they think will help them deflect
attention from incriminating facts when they're in trouble. I remember stopping a car for running a red light, and
the driver arguing that I had stopped him because he was
a black man driving a Mercedes. This was at night, so I had
no idea who was driving. The driver knew what he had
done, but he also knew he could hide behind an accusation
like that. I doubt these seasoned DOJ lawyers would believe
all the people in prison who claim to be innocent, but they
didn't hesitate to swallow every tale of woe from every citizen who says they were stopped on the street by a police
officer "for no reason."

In the report, FPD gets taken to task for incidents such as
one in which a citizen complains bitterly about being charged
with destruction of public property because of bloodstains
on a police uniform. Of course it sounds terrible if the police
wrote a guy up for bleeding. What isn't made clear is that this
person had become violent inside the police station and had
struck several officers, breaking the nose of one of them. The
report also talks a lot about our use of Tasers, although only
five of more than fifty officers in the department had a Taser
because of budget constraints. The whole point of Tasers, of
course, is to prevent hands-on engagement, and to give an

officer an alternative to deadly force. The DOJ describes an incident in which the report claims officers unjustly used a Taser on a man who was walking in the street and refused to move out of traffic. That man was in fact standing in the middle of an interstate highway, was physically powerful and intimidating, and, according to what the FPD officers reported, had thrown several of them around "like ragdolls." In the report, however, the Justice investigators describe him as "beginning to resist." The report is rife with similar examples of events being mischaracterized, giving the absolutely false impression of a pattern of recklessness on the part of the police. It's offensive to me, knowing how hard these officers worked and how seriously they took their jobs.

The list of misrepresentations goes on and on. The Justice Department scolds us for an allegedly inadequate system for hearing and addressing civilian complaints about interactions with police, while making no mention of the completely revised grievance process that I instituted, and about which I had provided them with information. The system was designed specifically to be transparent and make use of impartial public review.

The Justice Department titles another section of the report as follows: "FPD's Lack of Community Engagement Increases the Likelihood of Discriminatory Policing and Damages Public Trust." Here's yet another instance of the investigators stacking the deck with anonymous hearsay from people with something to gain by making the police look bad, while making no mention the of University of Missouri study that demonstrated resident confidence in the police at 76 percent; no mention that Ferguson was one of the few communities in the state that had shown steadily more favorable scores on the Racial Disparity Index issued by the state attorney general; no mention of the work we had done to hold public housing landlords to accountability; no mention of the nine neighborhood associations we helped establish, the neighborhood watch programs, the police volunteers, the Ferguson Youth Initiative, the alternative sentencing initiative, the forgiving of warrants, the community resource officers and school officers, nor any of the many other programs and efforts we had undertaken on our own initiative, to improve trust and quality of life in Ferguson. The DOJ also calls on us to increase the diversity on our force, even as it points out that "racial diversity does not necessarily increase community trust or improve officer conduct." The report writers choose not to acknowledge recent promotions of African American officers to high rank, nor the efforts made to hire more officers of color, nor the well-documented difficulty in doing so.

As I said at the beginning of this chapter, it's virtually impossible for me to cry foul as often as I feel the Department of Justice report demands. I feel like the more falsehoods and inconsistencies I point out, the more I sound like an obsessive madman. This report, however—with its direct and damning accusations based on evidence that would be thrown out of any court, its calculated bias, its incorrect and irresponsible labeling of practices as unlawful or unconstitutional, and its unsupported assertion that those practices had done harm to the community and its residents—had a devastating effect on Ferguson. The facts show that Ferguson was a town on the rise, a town that was doing better in virtually all measurable ways with community spirit, development, and overhaul of outmoded systems. By issuing this report, the Department of Justice stopped all that progress in its tracks. I don't fault anyone for trying to address concerns about policing or about systemic racism, but to sacrifice a good community full of committed people in the process—well, that's simply wrong.

It's clear to me that the activists in Eric Holder's Department of Justice had their sights set on problems in the criminal justice system that were much, much larger than the town of Ferguson, Missouri. The statutes and practices that were portrayed in the report as so outrageous are, in fact, standard in virtually every municipality in the country. The report describes them with no context, and in a deliberately prejudicial way, singling out the city, and laying all the blame at the feet of city management. Ferguson was a convenient scapegoat. Basically, the DOJ condemns the city for not spearheading wholesale criminal justice reform all on its own, with no resources and no support.

In my mind, the worst injustice perpetrated by the Justice Department is that it lays every sin at the feet of the police and the criminal justice system, which is a blatant case of mistaking a symptom for the disease. Everything about the DOJ's devastating condemnation of the Ferguson police and the Ferguson municipal court deflects the public's attention away from the real problems of concentrated and intractable poverty and all the decades of well-intentioned but mishandled public policy—from housing to education to public assistance programs—that have perpetuated it, and that nobody wants to take responsibility for, or even address. That's the work we all need to do, which leads us into the next chapter's discussion.

Chapter Eight

Blaming Police for a Broken Society

The conversation about policing has become so over-wrought in the last few years. It seems to me the best way to move forward is to try to come up with an understanding of the ideal function of police in our society, so that we can, together, establish a reasonable and achievable set of expectations for modern police forces.

Let's be honest: facts don't lie. No one can argue away the data that clearly shows that African Americans account for a wildly disproportionate number of arrests, street stops, use-of-force incidents, incarcerations, and other measurable events within our criminal justice system. At the same time, too many media images of people of color being beaten, or worse, by police have filled our screens. But we have to be very, very careful about concluding that all this is caused by racist police, or inherent racial bias in police practice or in the criminal justice system. Not only would that be mis-guided, it's dangerous, because blaming police for a great number of problems that society has dropped into the laps of law enforcement just gives us an easy scapegoat, and an easy excuse for continuing to shove all those problems back under the rug. We also have to take a hard look at exactly why so many people feel so much anger toward police. I believe that a lot of that is really disappointment and frustration over the failure of police to live up to the constantly growing demands put on them, demands that are by now completely unreasonable.

If we want to determine the proper role of police, it might help to look back at the origins of policing in this country. The great irony is that policing really began as a community-based enterprise, where a constable, sheriff, or other public safety officer was a constant presence in a small town or neighborhood. That officer would know the business owners, families, and children, and could be a resource to the citizens for all kinds of assistance. As the towns and cities grew, these officers were organized into municipal forces that were paid for and regulated by government. The job of law enforcement is simple: deter, detect, apprehend. Police officers sought to deter crime, to detect and investigate crime and its perpetrators when it occurred, and to apprehend criminals. There was a time when a beat cop could snatch up a misbehaving kid, give a scolding, and return the kid home to the parents. The same cop would be aware of newcomers or anything out of the ordinary.

It was that familiarity that helped maintain order and safety, and it is exactly the policing every law enforcement official wishes we could still do. We all try; I went out of my way in Ferguson to make it possible for our officers to become a part of the fabric of a neighborhood, but with con-stantly shrinking budgets and manpower it became next to impossible. In most parts of the country, even in densely populated urban centers, police are limited to car patrols, and are constantly in response mode rather than proactively making their presence known on foot patrols.

A great many rapid changes in our way of life made the beat cop obsolete. There were the great population shifts of the last century, first as people left the farmlands for cities and factory work, and then again when people streamed out of the cities into the suburbs. The population became mobile, with everybody moving around in cars, and police followed suit. Guns proliferated, and again, police kept up. New technology and the capacity to record and process tons of data enable government and law enforcement to identify patterns and trends, and so to predict where crime was most likely to occur. This led to more targeted patrols, which in turn evolved into the policy we call "hot spot" policing. As a simple example, when I first took over in Ferguson, one of the most common crimes was the theft of copper piping from abandoned buildings and houses. There was a lucrative resale market where thieves could unload their stolen metal. We focused patrol resources in those areas with the highest concentration of abandoned structures, and at the same time, investigated and eventually took down the scrap metal traffickers, attacking the problem from both ends.

I've tried to explain how this kind of strategy would eventually lead the police to beef up patrols in, for instance, an area with a lot of transient residents, where streets are overcrowded with cars, where cars themselves are often illegal or abandoned. Those areas are also likely to have higher unemployment, lower incomes, and the crime that usually thrives in that kind of environment. Nobody would argue with police assigning more resources to these areas of higher crime. But when those populations are predominantly people of color or immigrant communities, that will be reflected in all the law enforcement statistics. It's practically the definition of a vicious cycle. Worse, it provided critics with all the ammunition they need to argue that the data proves racism on the part of the police.

But as the world became more and more interconnected, the police—even small municipal police forces—suddenly had all kinds of new assignments on their plates. The drug trade reaches far beyond the local street corner, with every sale eventually traceable to sources across the country and across our borders. Beyond the devastation caused by drugs, local police have become the foot soldiers in national law enforcement efforts from immigration control to homeland security and domestic terrorism. In the course of my career, I've worked with agents from the FBI, DEA, ATF, and INS, sometimes all at once, as I did when running the drug task force in St. Louis. All local police share the public's desire to reestablish relationships and rebuild trust, but nobody wants to acknowledge that there are fewer and fewer cops with more and more responsibilities. It's hard to focus on starting a neighborhood association or organizing a youth athletic program when police are busy training for active-shooter scenarios, or searching out undocumented factory workers, or helping a federal agency track a suspected terrorist cell, or negotiating a truce between rival drug gangs.

You have to take a step back and look at the larger picture to understand the impact of all this on local policing. There was a time, not that long ago, when a municipal police chief could set policing priorities in a way that could maximize the force's value to the public. The chief and the officers could feel a sense of ownership and investment in those goals, which were based in their own experience and local knowledge. Now, however, with local police doing so much of the legwork for so many state and federal agencies, their marching orders come in large part from far-off bureaucrats, few of whom have any idea of what else the local police have on their plate at any given time. In many cases, the politicians and officials who are crying out for more community-centered policing are the same ones setting priorities for local police that leave little room for that community work.

Recently, especially since the national uproar about policing that erupted after the crisis in Ferguson in 2014, police across the country have had to shoulder an additional burden: it's become our primary job to undo all the effects of all these years of supposedly corrupt and oppressive policing. The nation seems to have collectively decided that everything about policing is fucked up, and while no one's quite sure how to do it, the police have been assigned with getting it un-fucked. We should do that while we're helping urban youth navigate their way to adulthood and nurturing a sense of neighborhood pride in our towns; while we're keeping churches, movie theaters, and shopping centers safe from mass killers with automatic weapons; while we're preventing fanatics from building bombs and blowing up airports; and while we're tracking down delinquent slumlords and intercepting drug shipments. You get the idea. It almost goes without saying that all these demands are piling up at the same time that police departments across the country are having to slash their budgets.

When police have time and manpower to engage in the contemporary version of "community policing," that, too, puts an enormously heavy burden on the average officer. A new officer today needs to be more worldly, more educated than in the past. The more a young recruit understands about psychology and sociology, the more sensitive and effective they're likely to be as a cop. You want people on your force who can recognize and diffuse a tense domestic situation, or distinguish between a serious mental health problem and a drug-altered mental state. On top of that, good policing requires a more specific understanding of history, of culture, and of people. Around St. Louis, for example, we arranged for officers to take classes in Bosnian history in order to better understand and serve the substantial Bosnian immigrant population in our area. In the same vein, two of the officers in my command taught a police academy course in understanding Islam. For the record, this was a good five years before events in Ferguson and elsewhere triggered a public outcry about out-of-touch police. It's just what we always did.

With all the uninformed talk about excessive force and police brutality, people would probably be surprised to know that the quality I looked for most in new police recruits was the ability to talk to people, to talk down a volatile situation. There's something uniquely ironic about police work: they are sworn to "serve and protect," but at the same time, cops are trained to physically subdue a suspect, to fight for their lives, and to kill. In fact, an officer has to accept that as a possible requirement of the job. At the same time, though, the burden on police to avoid violence is greater than it is on the civilian population. Police departments have to examine candidates very carefully, trying to discern anything that might indicate a person is too quick to violence or unable to effectively engage and influence people with words. That ability to talk is almost always a cop's best weapon.

Another experience from my own police career illustrates this point. Some years ago, I was part of a team dispatched to the scene of a standoff involving an armed man believed to be holding hostages in a house. My colleague, Al Eickhoff, who later became my assistant chief in Ferguson, was also part of that team. At one point, the gunman was lured outside. Al and I had entered the house at that point, and so were able to approach the man from behind. To reach him, we'd have to cross a small patch of the yard, a treacherous sprint given that he held a pistol in each hand. At the time, it seemed like all the other options were likely to result in the gunman being shot and killed. Al and I chose to make a run at the guy, and I was able to tackle and subdue him with no shots being fired. We were each awarded a Medal of Valor for that action, but I tell it here now not to boast about our heroism but to show the value placed by police on choosing nonlethal tactics. If there was any heroism that day, it was in the choice to take that suspect unharmed.

A good cop today is expected to be part priest, part family counselor, part teacher, and part warrior, but that's a very tough set of requirements to fulfill. Sadly, I believe that with police under the microscope as they currently are, and with the expectations of police becoming nearly impossible to meet, the public's sense of disappointment is going to continue to grow and the criticism will become even harsher. My greatest fear is that it's going to be harder and harder to attract good people to police work.

The current spin seems to be that young people are drawn to police work because they seek power and authority, an opportunity to somehow assert themselves or flex some muscles, but I think that portrayal misses the boat. We do want young people who are assertive, but in the same positive way that any organization seeks people who are confident and who believe in their capacity for making a difference. I'm reminded of the old saying, "Lead, follow, or get the hell out of the way." The best young officer candidates are the natural leaders, not egotists who think they should be the boss, but the people who can think on their feet, who are not afraid of inserting themselves into situations. We want the people who are problem-solvers, the ones who look for solutions when others are panicked or in despair. We want people who believe they can improve the quality of life in their community. We want people, as we teach them, who will "treat everyone like you'd want your mother to be treated." But even strong young people who fit that description may be reluctant to begin a career in which they themselves are considered at the start to be the problem.

I am a cop, a law enforcement professional. I spent my career training and studying, acquiring new knowledge and new skills, gaining experience and rising in rank until earning the title of chief. The commitment I made to "serve and protect" has taken on layers and layers of additional meaning since I first came on the job. I am not a policy expert. I have no training in social work or urban planning, education or economic development, and still, as a public servant and citizen, as well as a police officer, I've involved myself in various efforts in all of these different areas, not only because the public seems now to expect that from cops, but because these are ways in which I can have a positive impact.

Now the challenge for all of us in law enforcement is to set a clear path forward, to work with the activists, politicians, citizen groups, and other governmental agencies, first, to ratchet down the tension and hostility, and second, to create an atmosphere of mutual trust and shared purpose. I look back on everything we did in Ferguson with those goals in mind: not just the basic policing strategies like establishing community officers and school officers, but trying to effect real change by tracking down delinquent public housing landlords, forming neighborhood associations, sponsoring job fairs and volunteer programs, serving on commissions that attracted new businesses and jobs to the city and that revitalized the public parks, arranging community service sentencing alternatives in the municipal court, expunging fines and creating amnesty programs, and so much more. I can't even count the number of parades, ball games, fairs, block parties, and church picnics that either I or one of my officers attended; it was our town, too. Until everything blew up in August 2014, the community leaders and city officials worked comfortably across racial lines on all of these efforts. The only thing that mattered was a person's commitment to making Ferguson a town to be admired.

I understand now that whatever we did as police, it would never have been enough. Let's look again at how the US Department of Justice defines community policing:

> Community policing is a philosophy that promotes organizational strategies, which support the systematic use of partnerships and problem-solving techniques, to proactively address the immediate conditions that give rise to public safety issues, such as crime, social disorder, and fear of crime.

It is a noble idea, and I haven't come across many ranking law enforcement officials who wouldn't do whatever they could to make it all happen. But I wonder what the policymakers in Washington think a police department in a small city has in its toolbox, or what resources the Department of Justice thinks it's providing, that makes it possible for cops on the street to "proactively address the immediate conditions that give rise to public safety issues," specifically "social disorder"? There is absolutely no doubt in my mind about the immediate condition that primarily gives rise to social disorder: poverty, pure and simple. Concentrated, intractable poverty. Institutionalized, generational poverty.

Poverty destroys families, traps young people in a never-ending spiral of hopelessness, and drives them to seek not only money to live on, but self-esteem, from all manner of misguided and criminal activities, or to escape into a haze of drugs, alcohol, and random violence. To say so is not to blame the lifestyle of any particular racial or ethnic group, or to invoke a stereotyped image of burnt-out inner cities. Americans tend to forget that there is more rural poverty in this country than there is in metropolitan areas. And those areas, whether it's Appalachia or the Southwest or the upper Midwest, face many of the same consequences as the troubled urban areas: a high percentage of single-parent households, lower high school graduation rates, and a thriving illegal drug trade. Wherever those conditions exist, crime follows, but it's in the cities and the inner suburbs where too many people are crammed into too little space, and where poverty sits right next to unimaginable wealth, that violent crime and property crime flourishes most.

If unrelenting poverty is the primary condition underlying social disorder and crime, there are two basic questions we have to ask. First, how did police become almost the central focus of any discussion of social problems and inequality? And second, what role is law enforcement expected to play in alleviating poverty? As stunned as I was by what I read in the Department of Justice's report on Ferguson, the fact is that I was just as stunned by what wasn't in there. Did the report take the Department of Housing and Urban Development to task for mismanagement—or in some cases, total lack of management—in the public housing projects in Ferguson? Did it mention the Education Department's responsibility for the underfunded schools that had trouble engaging Ferguson's young people and preparing them for life as adults and citizens? Did it mention Health and Human Services and the lack of access to first-rate health care, or any of the other state and federal agencies that failed to support and promote the local economy or rebuild infrastructure? Of course not. No, the DOJ laid all the problems of Ferguson's African Americans at the feet of a concocted brutal police department and a greedy, racist court system.

By convincing the public that police—in Ferguson or anywhere else—are reflexively racist, the Department of Justice has unwittingly thrown fat on the fire and made it more difficult to carry out the basic tasks of law enforcement. Do police officers engage in racial profiling? Yes, it happens. I learned it firsthand as a teenager, driving to a music rehearsal with my brother and a close African American friend. A cop pulled us over and asked, "Does your mother know who you're with?" It was obvious he wasn't talking to our friend, Charles.

"Yes, sir," I replied. "She just made him dinner." I had to contain my anger, but Charles remained pleasant and calm throughout the encounter because this was nothing new to him. He was used to being pulled over for no reason other than the color of his skin. The experience shocked me and changed me forever, and I incorporated these feelings into my work and my leadership in policing.

The public also has to understand that what appears to be racial or ethnic profiling is often something else. When I ran the drug task force in St. Louis, we developed a very deep awareness of behaviors common to drug mules. If the team assigned surveillance to particular travelers at a motel, for example, it would be because of telltale signs having to do with the amount of luggage, the pattern of leaving and returning to the room, phone use, room service, and so on, not because the travelers appeared to be of a particular ethnic group. If you're trafficking drugs from south of the border, for instance, you're probably smart enough to know to employ people who don't fit any profile anyway—families, senior citizens, etc.

As an experienced policeman, I know that traffic stops generally result from a driver's suspicious behavior behind the wheel rather than his or her skin color. But as a man who lives in the real world, I know that's not always true, and that's created its own law enforcement challenges. Consider this possibility: a cop witnesses a car drive straight through a red light at an intersection and he pulls the car over. The car is a high-end import, and when the driver rolls down his window, the officer sees that the driver is African American.

"Do you know why I pulled you over?" the cop asks.

"Yeah, you pulled me over because I'm a black man driving a Mercedes."

Does that sound far-fetched? It isn't; I know it happened because, as I mentioned in the previous chapter, I was the cop who pulled that guy over. Once a citizen makes an allegation like that, regardless of whether it's true, the officer's hands are tied. What would you do if you were the cop? Do you write the guy up, knowing you might end up defending yourself in a grievance hearing or maybe even a lawsuit? Do you let the guy off this one time, knowing that the next red light he runs could cost someone their life? And what's the message you send when you let someone off for a relatively minor traffic offense? That police are decent people that you can work with, or that police are running scared so you can take advantage of them? Or maybe they're just lax at enforcing the law. What happens if the next time it's maybe a question of public drunkenness or someone caught smoking a harmless joint? It's a slippery slope, and it seems obvious that police just have to do their job, but the public has to acknowledge how much harder it has become to do that job. This is one of the many ways in which the Department of Justice undermined its own mission. As sincere as the DOJ was about trying to address some real issues of inequality in the criminal justice system, when it made Ferguson a scapegoat with an exaggerated and sometimes fabricated case, it emboldened lawbreakers and stripped police of the authority they need to do the job, all with the net effect of making the public less safe.

There's no doubt that African Americans and other minorities have been pulled over for driving fancy cars, or for driving in predominantly white neighborhoods. I don't question that they've been shadowed in department stores or discouraged from buying homes in certain communities. All Americans, not only police officers, have to do a better job of recognizing and correcting our unconscious biases. Ironically, racial sensitivity training, to specifically address such biases, is required of all law enforcement professionals, which is a lot more than can be said about most Americans' jobs. I'll wager that cops are more attuned to various forms of profiling than average citizens. I could even make the case that white cops in some communities—Ferguson being one of them—spend more time with, and are more sensitive to, the challenges facing minorities in troubled neighborhoods than the average white citizen. I'd even argue that those cops' understanding of those communities is more nuanced, and includes the majority of residents who we know to be as hardworking and committed as anybody else, and who want to work with police and city government for a safer, more prosperous environment. That's because the cops are there every day, serving and protecting.

And still, we had to sit and listen to a Justice Department official tell us to back off and not do the best job we can do protecting a community from imminent rioting because it might look bad in the face of three hundred years of history. And then we had to watch our department, and most of the city government, dismantled because the Justice Department falsely and cynically portrayed our police and courts as a corrupt money-making operation. People get into police work and public service because they want to be part of the solution, not part of the problem, and in my five years in Ferguson, I believe that's exactly how we all tried to operate.

What I also believe is that by identifying bad policing as the central problem, the country is singling out an easy, convenient, high-profile scapegoat as a way of avoiding the more catastrophic problems facing poor people, of all races, but especially poor people of color. It allows society basically to kick the can down the road, until the only people left to blame are the cops and courts and jails, who just can't seem to clean it all up as neatly as everybody wants. You can replace or retrain every police officer in America until you have a perfect, spotless police force, but that wouldn't do a thing to alleviate poverty and inequality. It wouldn't redistribute education resources so that towns and cities with dwindling tax revenues could help their young people start off on the same footing as kids from more wealthy suburbs. It wouldn't build or restore industry or provide job training or help people start small businesses. It wouldn't fix broken public assistance programs in housing, or food or health or income subsidies, which seem to trap good people in a cycle of dependence instead of offering them ways out. It wouldn't put broken homes back together, and it wouldn't rid the streets of the guns and drugs that tempt young people who feel they've run out of options.

These are the gravest threats to public safety. Police officers are trained to deter, detect, and apprehend criminals.

The crimes they deal with are the symptoms, not the disease, but that hasn't stopped me or most of the cops I've worked with from recognizing the disease and doing what we can to treat it. Now, given this huge gap between the enormous expectations placed upon police and the minimal resources at their disposal, and given the environment of hostility in which they work, how can police continue to have a positive influence on the communities in which they live and work?

For all the different ways that our force involved itself in the community, I recognize that there are ways in which we can go deeper. It starts with the police seeing themselves as more than just the last line of defense, but as a frontline resource. We don't have to settle for being primarily reactive, but can bring our experience in, and knowledge of, the communities we serve to bear in a proactive way. For example, I used to meet regularly with the superintendent of Ferguson's high school and other officials from the school district. Those meetings, while definitely a step in the right direction, focused almost exclusively on security issues—policing for drugs, weapons, fights, etc. Occasionally we would discuss what else a school resource officer might bring to the table—lead a seminar on job hunting or some other aspect of citizenship, or possibly help organize some extracurricular event or activity.

It occurs to me now that my time with the school officials might have been better spent by sharing my department's observations of those kids' lives outside of the school environment. I could talk about absenteeism in the context of inadequate childcare for parents working multiple jobs. I could tell the educators about the homes where there was no real history of employment. We could talk about drug and alcohol or abuse problems in some households that almost certainly affected a kid's performance in school. The fact of the matter is that there are kids in our school district whose families may be hiding the fact that they are literally homeless.

The point is that cops engage with the community all day every day. We should be sitting down with educators and explaining what we see as gaps that need to be filled in some kids' knowledge or understanding of citizenship, so that the schools can create programs and curriculums that might address those specific needs. Expanding on that idea, why can't we share our knowledge with other public agencies, like the housing office or HHS or Social Security? Each of those departments is as understaffed and underfunded as the police—a situation that's only likely to get worse in the near future—so the best thing we can do is come together and pool our resources, share our knowledge and insights, and set policies and strategies on a local level, taking all these factors and concerns into account.

Police and other law enforcement professionals have always done this, usually on an informal, ad hoc basis, as have so many other people who work in public service professions. But think of the value that could be added if this were officially part of the job description. Think of all the young people currently turned off by police work who might reconsider if they knew that people understood the job to be about leadership and community development, rather than just fighting a losing battle against social disorder and public hostility. Think also of how that kind of proactive engagement could change public perception and show the public what I've always known—that police want nothing more than to be on the front lines of positive change.

It's a tricky business for someone like me to offer my thoughts on what's needed or on how people might improve their own lives in the communities I serve. I know how much good there is in even the worst-off neighborhoods. There are families that remain committed to their neighbors and communities and to each other, and organizations and institutions that provide structure and support and stability. No matter how many resources there are, it's still the people themselves who either engage, or don't. My work has given me ample opportunity to observe, and sometimes those observations reveal patterns, but I know that generalizing about groups or communities is a minefield. What happens if I say that my experience shows that too many of the kids who get into enough trouble—trouble that leads to contact with police—have a poorly developed sense of personal responsibility? I can tell you what did happen: the US Department of Justice told me I placed way too much emphasis on personal responsibility, making me just another racist cop.

Everybody needs opportunity, and everybody needs desire. What I believe is that given love and attention, at home and from the community that surrounds them, people are going to have desire. Desire doesn't survive long in the absence of opportunity, and opportunity is stifled by stacking people on top of each other in the warehouses of hopelessness that public housing usually turns out to be.

Chapter 9

Aftermath

When the Department of Justice made its bomb-shell report on Ferguson public in March 2015, seven months after the shooting, I immediately knew my time as FPD chief was up. There would never be any peace for me or for Ferguson if I remained in my job. I could see that I'd be spending all my time trying to prove the DOJ wrong, and defending myself and my department from their outrageous accusations. At the same time, Ferguson's political leadership was coming to the same conclusion. John Shaw, the city manager, let me know he'd be stepping down. He and the mayor, James Knowles, explained that with the city council changing over as well, we'd all have less support there than in the past. The DOJ report also effectively negated Missouri's "just cause" law, which had protected municipal police chiefs from firings for political reasons.

I made my decision to resign, but gave myself a week to help my assistant chief, Al Eickhoff, make the transition into the chief's spot, which he would be occupying on an interim basis. Hoping to reward one of the few journalists who had covered the story with fairness and integrity, I gave a heads-up to Christine Byers, a reporter at the *St. Louis Post-Dispatch*, and she broke it in that paper. The public, and many in the press, had been calling for my head for so long that we all believed the announcement of my resignation would have a calming effect, maybe even cause the fever to break. We could not have been more wrong.

The very night that the story broke, a major protest materialized at the Ferguson police headquarters and there was nothing peaceful about it. Two police officers were shot that night while they defended the station house. These were the first serious injuries to result from direct acts of violence— the first serious injuries of any kind, in fact—since the protests and riots began, and ironically, they occurred on the night when we thought we'd see the tensions abate. The two officers, one shot in the face and the other in the shoulder, survived and are okay now; the shooter was apprehended, tried, and convicted.

For me, the resignation actually turned up the heat. The press hounded me more aggressively than ever, chasing me wherever I went and phoning me virtually nonstop. I started receiving calls from around the world—that's how big the Ferguson story had grown. I seriously began to wonder what the future held for me.

I had gotten a pretty unsettling glimpse of a possible future a few weeks earlier, when I accepted an invitation to appear at a "Roundtable on Policing" at the Harvard Law School, which I have alluded to earlier in this book. James Knowles and I traveled to Cambridge, Massachusetts, for the event, looking forward to the chance to share our perspective, and discuss the fallout from the Ferguson experience with academics and leaders at one of the country's most respected institutions. In retrospect, I maybe should have noted that the roundtable was sponsored by the Charles Hamilton Houston Institute for Race and Justice within Harvard's law school, and realized that the discussion would follow the narrative of racial injustice, but James and I both remained optimistic and excited about the opportunity.

In the days before the event, which had originally been intended to be a pretty small, intimate affair, the number of requests for attendance shot up and the event was moved to a four-hundred-seat auditorium. When we arrived, every seat was full, and the aisles and stairs were packed with people standing or sitting on the floor. On every seat had been placed a one-page flyer—put there not by the organizers of the event but by a group called the Harvard Ferguson Action Committee—that condemned the university for allowing Mayor Knowles and me to speak on campus, and asserting that the two of us were "human rights abusers" and should resign. About me, the flyer stated, "Ferguson Police Chief Thomas Jackson has acted against international human rights standards in his response to Michael Brown's murder and through his use of tear gas, rubber bullets, and other violent tactics against peaceful protests." As has been documented by the Department of Justice itself, Michael Brown was not murdered, and at no time were violent tactics used against peaceful protesters. Truth was apparently not a concern of these righteous seekers of justice.

It only got worse from there. On the dais with us were two organizer/activists from an organization called Peace Keepers St. Louis, a law professor from Saint Louis University named Justin Hansford, and Derecka Purnell, a Harvard law student who said she grew up in and around Ferguson, and had gone there to take part in the protests.

The attacks on me started immediately. Ms. Purnell made a show of turning her back on James and me, claiming that she didn't want to sit with people responsible for guns pointed in her face. People in the audience shouted insults at us and demanded our resignations, then shouted even louder when I tried to explain that I didn't believe I'd be helping my community by quitting and dumping the problem in someone else's lap. A Ferguson resident, a businessman who had helped arrange our travel to Cambridge, tried to offer a balanced and accurate description of the town, but he, too, was shouted down.

When Professor Hansford spoke, he told the audience that I—he singled me out by name—had left Michael Brown's body lying in the street for hours deliberately, as a warning about what could happen to other people. I remember the shock I felt hearing a man who held the title "professor" say such a despicable thing as if it were true. The event quickly fell apart with everybody shouting and nobody listening. One of the activists got hold of a microphone and just started shouting and cursing, calling me "motherfucker" and other names. What was supposed to be a civil exchange of ideas and opinions, an open conversation at an institution renowned for its intellectual integrity, ended in pandemonium with campus police escorting us out for our own safety.

The Harvard event was an absolute low point for me, but to my great surprise, the experience ended on a couple of positive notes. For one thing, I met a man named Gabriel Baez, the nephew of Eric Garner, the man who died while being arrested by a New York City police officer. Here was a man with a deep personal connection to the issues under discussion, but rather than vent his rage, he struck me as thoughtful and compassionate, explaining that he had come to the conference hoping to help prevent such deaths in the future. That was why we were all there, I had thought, and I appreciated the time Baez spent talking with me and engaging with the issues.

After the police ushered us out of the building, we were taken to dinner at Legal Sea Foods, the Boston landmark. At the table next to us was Bruce Franks Jr., the St. Louis organizer and activist who had lost it on me back in the auditorium. In this friendlier setting, he was much calmer and more relaxed, and was willing not only to talk but also to listen. We had an open and productive exchange about Ferguson and about policing, during which, Franks told me, "I'm not sorry about what I said, but I am sorry about the way I said it." That meant a lot to me, reminding me that when we can get past the emotion, real dialogue is possible.

Franks and I stayed in touch well after that night, one of the silver linings in the cloud that hung over me then. Back in Ferguson, we worked together helping with the town-wide cleanup once the protests ended. Franks even helped start a recruitment program, hoping to interest young African American men to get involved with police work. Still bearing the gang tattoos of a life he left behind, he ran for state representative in the last election, and although he lost narrowly at first, he was declared the winner later, after part of the original vote tally was invalidated.

Engaged residents like Franks would be more important than ever to the future of Ferguson after the Justice Department was through with us. Once they completed their report, the DOJ and the city leadership had to negotiate some kind of agreement over what would happen next. What would Ferguson do to address the issues—real or not—that Justice laid out for us? The result was the consent decree signed by both sides in the spring of 2015. This document features a lot of language about the willingness of all the parties to work together to reach an amicable solution to alleged problems, and about the willingness of the Ferguson leadership to pro-actively participate. The reality was somewhat more compli-cated, as it usually is. The consent decree was pushed through by the DOJ, and signed reluctantly by the city once it realized that Ferguson just didn't have the financial resources to fight things out in court. The city wouldn't have the resources to do what the consent decree required of it, and the leaders realized soon enough that they didn't have much chance of improving the deal, even if they sued.

As far as I'm concerned, the consent decree just added insult to injury. The Justice Department lawyers filled it with condescending language designed to give the impression that they were sharing their wisdom with us know-nothings, when all they really did was put into words obvious prin-ciples that we already believed in, and were already acting on in the best way possible, given our resources. The DOJ knew all that, of course, but had consciously left it all out of their initial report. The very first line of the consent decree says that the federal government and the city of Ferguson enter into the agreement "with the shared recognition that the ability of a police department to protect the community it serves is only as strong as the relationship it has with that community." As if that had never occurred to anybody on my police force. The consent decree goes in this vein, beating us over the head with the obvious.

The decree also reiterates that "the Report documents DOJ's finding of a number of patterns or practices of uncon-stitutional conduct and details DOJ's concerns about a number of Ferguson's police and court policies and prac-tices," although in language that sidesteps the point that no court with the actual authority to declare anything unconstitutional ever did so and no such practices were ever proven except through the one-sided stack of hearsay presented by the Justice Department itself. I guess we were supposed to be happy the consent decree included a sentence acknowledging that Ferguson police officers "often work under difficult circumstances, risking their physical safety and well-being for the public good." At least the report acknowledges that the city of Ferguson does not agree with all the findings and requirements of the DOJ, and that its signing of the agreement does not in any way constitute an acknowledgement of any guilt or liability.

All the consent decree did was cement all the negative effects on the lives of Ferguson residents that the initial report had set in motion. Even if the city could carry them all out, the steps it had to take would strip away resources and directly cause a decrease in the level of public safety. During my tenure, we had gotten the police force up to a strength of fifty-five officers, but as of this writing that number has fallen below forty. The Department of Justice explicitly intended the steps outlined in the consent decree to facilitate more community engagement, but the first effect of a reduced force is a decrease in fruitful interactions between police and the public. Money for additional (and superfluous, in my opinion) oversight staff, would have to be redirected from necessary projects involving infrastructure, and from festivals, picnics, and other community events that were designed for no other reason than to improve community engagement.

One of the more painful lessons for me has been about the fragility of some relationships between social groups and ethnic groups, but also between individuals. I thought I had a pretty realistic, clear-eyed understanding of the racial and socioeconomic issues in Ferguson, and while I continue to believe that tensions were greatly exaggerated by activists from outside of town, by the media, and by the federal investigators, I wasn't prepared for how quickly so many friendships and productive working relationships were cast aside.

With the town suddenly in a fishbowl, optics took priority, but on a more deeply personal level. People started to feel like they had to choose sides, or more to the point, many African Americans whom my wife and I had known for years in Ferguson no longer wanted to be identified with me or with other white residents. Dwayne James, of the Ferguson city council, became distant, and this was a man who had never hesitated to enlist me for projects and events around town and to work in genuine partnership with me. I considered him a friend. Charles Glenn, a well-known entertainment figure in St. Louis who has been my friend since we were teenagers, told me that the pastor at his church had started saying terrible things about me from the pulpit. It got bad enough that Charles chose to leave that church, and continued to defend me.

I watched as the troubles in Ferguson tore families apart. My personal assistant at the FPD, Mary Simmons, an African American woman whom I had depended on throughout my time as chief, remained steadfast at a great personal cost. She didn't make a big deal about it, but I knew that she was getting a lot of flak from her family, many of whom were badgering her about "working for that man." As I understand it, nobody ever had a problem with me, or with Mary working for the FPD, before the shooting of Michael Brown. Everything changed after that. It was us against them with no tolerance for anyone in the middle. Confrontation was valued over cooperation. Other residents who worked with the police department through our VIP (Volunteers in Policing) program, cut their ties with us.

But nobody in Ferguson had it worse than the African American police officers on the scene, whose commitment to duty was rewarded by being singled out as traitors and being subjected to vicious and personal threats and abuse whenever they hit the street in uniform.

As the dust has slowly settled, I've continued to see positive developments coming out of Ferguson's ordeal. I'm extremely fortunate to have been embraced by the law enforcement community around the country, and around the world, for that matter. Skeptical readers may dismiss the importance of support coming from other cops, but it has meant a great deal. After being torn apart in the press and becoming estranged from many people I once thought of as friends, it was hard not to question myself, to wonder what I did to deserve that kind of treatment when I had only been doing my duty. To be invited to speak to police organizations and associations in so many different cities, to be welcomed and treated as a professional, to be respected by the people who best understand both my accomplishments and the devastating costs to me—it's hard to describe how much that helped restore my own sense of personal dignity.

I think these other cops appreciated that I had not only stood up for the cops on my force, and had chosen to endure months and months of public abuse rather than abandon my post and let my officers down, but also that I had stood up for police in general. They respected the fact that I hadn't let the critics and naysayers back me down, and I never gave in to the crazy narratives in the media. At the annual

"Cop Week" in Washington, DC, I was treated like a real celebrity. One cop summed it up: "You're America's police chief." I have patches—gifts of great significance among cops—from police departments and other agencies all over America, and even an English "bobby" hat. It was truly a humbling experience.

But as honored and humbled as I was to get such genuinely warm treatment from fellow officers, it wasn't nearly as important as the opportunities to help bridge the divide between police and the public we had sworn to serve. In New York City, I saw both sides of that equation. I was treated to a tour of One Police Plaza and of the NYPD's amazing high-tech command center, and I had a sit-down with the deputy commissioner of police. Then I was honored by an invitation to participate in a program there called Operation Conversation: Cops & Kids, founded and run by Dr. Lenora Fulani. This program puts inner-city kids together with the police working in their communities, and uses performance-based workshops to create dialogue and understanding between them. The workshops put on by this group are moving, inspiring, and a lot of fun. The highlight was a gala event at the Apollo Theater in Harlem, attended by the newest graduating class from the New York Police Academy. The standing ovation I received on stage at the Apollo, from both city kids and city cops, made me feel like the important conversation we were having about policing and race and crime and poverty in American—the conversation that had started on the streets of Ferguson—was starting to move in a positive direction.

Epilogue

Since Michael Brown's death and the uproar that followed in the summer of 2014, the nation has been engaged in a painful process of reevaluating the purpose and the practice of policing. But to understand what got us to that moment, we have to look way beyond policing. It means examining not just the many other social and cultural factors and governmental policies that affect our cities, but really, the entire history of our country.

In the heat of the moment, a police officer can only respond to the immediate circumstances around him or her. Wouldn't it be great if we could stop and consider the generations of frustration that preceded a spontaneous outbreak of anger and violence? That's what the Department of Justice would have us do, and as noble an intention as it is, it's not really feasible. It is, however, the conversation that we have to have as a nation.

I've been going through a similar process of reflection, on a more personal level, trying to look objectively at my career and at the work we did in Ferguson to make policing more responsive and effective, and more closely woven into the fabric of the community. In many ways, that process began as soon as I took over as chief, four years before the shooting and the riots. In the years since everything blew up, however, I've been presented with a flood of criticism, ranging from people screaming in my face on the streets of Ferguson or in a lecture hall at Harvard, to long investigative reports in the media and the meticulously detailed and spectacularly wrongheaded Department of Justice report. I've never claimed to be perfect in my job, and I'm actually grateful to have had the opportunity to look into each of those specific criticisms. And what I found upon close examination absolutely confirmed my faith and confidence in the people I work with and the job we do as police.

Can we do better? Certainly. Can we make use of the lessons learned in Ferguson and elsewhere? Absolutely. But at no time, when I was able to calmly evaluate the criticism and arguments against the practice of policing, did I conclude that the critics had gotten it completely right. I never thought, "Wow, how come none of us professionals ever thought of that? How could we know so little about the work we do, or the people with whom we interact, every single day?"

One thing we can all do better is communicate. Police have to be absolutely transparent about the practices and procedures, not only in isolated moments of crisis but also concerning big-picture issues of policy. I did everything I could to be open and to reduce the distance between citizens and police in Ferguson. During the riots, police routinely made public announcements about what kind of protests would be accommodated and what activities would be deemed a threat to public safety and so trigger a police response. Clear communication is always at the top of the list of action steps for police officers. But police and courts and citizens can and must all work together to establish police priorities, to assign and distribute resources. Everybody has to agree on the ground rules, so that there can be no surprise, no recriminations after the fact.

Maybe there's some irony in the fact that the explosion of social media, which helped create so much of the tension during the riots, can actually be a force for positive change going forward. Police, and all community leaders, can harness social media just as effectively as the protesters in Ferguson did, speaking directly to citizens, opening up processes and procedures, explain actions and decisions, and preparing the public for the unexpected. Police already use social media to issue what are called "reverse 911s" that alert people to danger or ask for assistance, but the internet offers countless opportunities to improve communications that we are only now beginning to explore.

I learned about the importance of optics and appearances. For instance, everyone in law enforcement knows that rescue vehicles are not tanks, or even military vehicles. Now, though, I'm sensitive to the fact that an imposing, armored vehicle rolling toward an agitated crowd can be very frightening. And if there's a rifleman sitting on the roof, as is the correct defensive protocol when such a vehicle is used, that is likely to be perceived as aggressive and intimidating. The same is of course true for most defensive measures that police have adopted. In a nation raised on images of the Imperial stormtroopers from *Star Wars*, a squadron of police wearing riot helmets with face masks and carrying shields is not going to be a comforting sight for most people. But if we ask police to be the heroic protectors of public safety, aren't we obligated to protect their safety too? We wouldn't send soldiers onto the battlefield with inadequate protection, so why would we send cops into a violent situation unprepared? Police dogs, tear gas, the very act of officers linking together in a defensive formation around a building, any of that is likely to remind citizens of some of the worst moments in American history—union riots, the civil rights clashes, anti-war protests, etc.—when the police were seen to be the faceless enforcers of intolerant policies and practices.

It's not that nobody in law enforcement had ever thought of any of that before the Ferguson riots. Police weigh the possible ramifications of every step before taking it. It surprises me that anyone would think we don't. We have to be aware of the potential of any tactic to inadvertently escalate tensions instead of calming things down. It's not always easy, or even possible, to think of every possible outcome. Often, there just isn't time, if events are unfolding quickly and circumstances change by the minute. And, police don't have unlimited options. There are only so many tools to choose from in our tool kit, but every effort is always made to think several moves ahead, to try to be prepared for problems before they crop up.

The paramilitary structure of modern policing is all I've ever known. It makes sense that leaders in law enforcement need to be very sensitive to the culture and warrior mentality that can easily grow out of that kind of organization. The fact remains, however, that America is basically armed to the teeth. Guns and drugs have spread like viruses, and violent crime, whether it's a gang war, a mass shooting in a public place, or a case of domestic battery involving two people in the privacy of their home, is absolutely everywhere. If the mission of police is to protect public safety, we don't really have a choice but to keep training them appropriately, to fight, to subdue, to shoot and even to kill, if they are to succeed.

But that is only one aspect of the life of a cop. If nothing else comes out of this experience, we can at least take away the acknowledgement that even though this loosely defined set of skills and practices that people call "community policing" is now and has always been a fundamental part of a cop's job, it has probably been a secondary priority. It's the stuff that committed cops do if and when they aren't focused on their primary mission of "deter, detect, and apprehend." It's the stuff they get pulled off their normal patrols to do, or do on their own time after their shifts are over. Money and resources are dwindling nationwide, and I don't think anyone wants to see crime rates go up because cops have been reassigned to duties with less immediately tangible results. At the same time, it's reasonable to believe that if they had the time, police could involve themselves in activities that would indirectly reduce crime, such as cleaning up the management and operation of public housing, or finding or creating volunteer opportunities for at-risk youth.

Maybe, however, we could come to a universal agreement that these activities should be an equal priority for police departments, instead of something they'll focus on when time allows. That represents a much bigger shift in public policy than people want to admit. If, as the Department of Justice asserts, community policing involves building partnerships in a community that can address the conditions that give rise to social disorder, are local, state, and federal governments prepared to provide the resources to accomplish that? Are they prepared to acknowledge that agencies and departments already exist that have aspects of that as their primary missions, and that finding money for police departments to staff up and make that possible would almost certainly mean siphoning money from those other departments?

At the end of the day, I believe the public has to realize that police are not the source of poverty, inequality, or racism. Historically, police are the ones left to clean up the messes created by those conditions. But cops, are in fact, engaged with those issues, directly or indirectly, every day. They are trained to cope with them, to be culturally aware and sensitive to the impact of those social problems on the lives of citizens. And since an ounce of prevention is worth a pound of cure—in policing as in everything else—cops have looked for ways to head off crime and disorder by strengthening ties between people, either one-on-one as community resource officers on foot patrol or by organizing neighborhood groups. They've always done so because that's the kind of people who become cops. The ones who want to find solutions and lead others in bringing about change—the people who have dedicated—and risked—their lives to create more unified and productive communities, as part of a stronger and more compassionate country.

All that is why I continue to say, "Let cops be cops."

Appendix

While some have quietly come around to the understanding that Michael Brown's death was not the result of police brutality or even police misconduct, too many Americans are still deeply invested in the "hands up, don't shoot" mythology. The detailed report issued by the FBI (a division of the Department of Justice), after months of careful examination, has been available to the public for a very long time*, but I believe that very few have taken the time to read it. The FBI's report is a model of precise, objective, and exhaustive investigative work.

It is important that the public understands a few facts about the reports issued by the Department of Justice. First, the two documents—the FBI investigation into the actual shooting and the DOJ Civil Rights Division's "pattern-or-practice" report—were prepared simultaneously, in the same amount of time, despite the fact that one dealt with events that happened in the space of a few minutes while the

---

* justice.gov/sites/default/files/opa/press-releases/attachments/
2015/03/04/ferguson_police_department_report_1.pdf

other dealt with decades of behavior of an entire community over multiple generations. Furthermore, the FBI's report exonerating Officer Darren Wilson was released on the same day as the pattern-or-practice report condemning Ferguson. It was overshadowed, receiving a fraction of the press coverage, and therefore nearly lost on most people.

Following is an excerpt from the Introduction to the FBI's report on the shooting. I include it here so readers can understand the care and professionalism that went into the report. It outlines the relevant laws and legal standards, the purpose and goals, the investigative procedures, the standards for gathering and evaluating evidence, and the process by which it reached its conclusions.

The Department conducted an extensive investigation into the shooting of Michael Brown. Federal authorities reviewed physical, ballistic, forensic, and crime scene evidence; medical reports and autopsy reports, including an independent autopsy performed by the United States Department of Defense Armed Forces Medical Examiner Service ("AFMES"); Wilson's personnel records; audio and video recordings; and internet postings. FBI agents, St. Louis County Police Department ("SLCPD") detectives, and federal prosecutors and prosecutors from the St. Louis County Prosecutor's Office ("county prosecutors") worked cooperatively to both independently and jointly interview more than 100 purported eyewitnesses and other individuals claiming to have relevant information. SLCPD detectives conducted an initial canvass of the area on the day of the shooting. FBI agents then independently canvassed more than 300 residences to locate and interview additional witnesses. Federal and local authorities collected cellular phone data, searched social media sites, and tracked down dozens of leads from community members and dedicated law enforcement email addresses and tip lines in an effort to investigate every possible source of information.

The principles of federal prosecution, set forth in the United States Attorneys' Manual ("USAM"), require federal prosecutors to meet two standards in order to seek an indictment. First, we must be convinced that the potential defendant committed a federal crime. *See* USAM § 9-27.220 (a federal prosecution should be commenced only when an attorney for the government "believes that the person's conduct constitutes a federal offense"). Second, we must also conclude that we would be likely to prevail at trial, where we must prove the charges beyond a reasonable doubt. *See* USAM § 9-27.220 (a federal prosecution should be commenced only when "the admissible evidence will probably be sufficient to sustain a conviction"); Fed R. Crim P. 29(a) (prosecution must present evidence sufficient to sustain a conviction). Taken together, these standards require the Department to be convinced both that a federal crime occurred and that it can be proven beyond a reasonable doubt at trial.

In order to make the proper assessment under these standards, federal prosecutors evaluated physical, forensic, and potential testimonial evidence in the form of witness accounts. As detailed below, the physical and forensic evidence provided federal prosecutors with a benchmark against which to measure the credibility of each witness account, including that of Darren Wilson. We compared individual witness accounts to the physical and forensic evidence, to other credible witness accounts, and to each witness's own prior statements made throughout the investigations, including the proceedings before the St. Louis County grand jury ("county grand jury"). We worked with federal and local law enforcement officers to interview witnesses, to include reinterviewing certain witnesses in an effort to evaluate inconsistencies in their accounts and to obtain more detailed information. In so doing, we assessed the witnesses' demeanor, tone, bias, and ability to accurately perceive or recall the events of August 9, 2014. We credited and determined that a jury would appropriately credit those witnesses whose accounts were consistent with the physical evidence and consistent with other credible witness accounts. In the case of witnesses who made multiple statements, we compared those statements to determine whether they were materially consistent with each other and considered the timing and circumstances under which the witnesses gave the statements. We did not credit and determined that a jury appropriately would not credit those witness accounts that were contrary to the physical and forensic evidence, significantly inconsistent with other credible witness accounts, or significantly inconsistent with that witness's own prior statements.

Based on this investigation, the Department has concluded that Darren Wilson's actions do not constitute prosecutable violations under the applicable federal criminal civil rights statute, 18 U.S.C. § 242, which prohibits uses of deadly force that are "objectively unreasonable," as defined by the United States Supreme Court. The evidence, when viewed as a whole, does not support the conclusion that Wilson's uses of deadly force were "objectively unreasonable" under the Supreme Court's definition. Accordingly, under the governing federal law and relevant standards set forth in the USAM, it is not appropriate to present this matter to a federal grand jury for indictment, and it should therefore be closed without prosecution.

Next, here is the FBI's official summary of its findings and conclusions that demonstrate the falseness of the narrative that took over the country in the summer and fall of 2014.

II. Summary of the Evidence, Investigation, and Applicable Law

A. Summary of the Evidence

Within two minutes of Wilson's initial encounter with Brown on August 9, 2014, FPD officers responded to the scene of the shooting, and subsequently turned the matter over to the SLCPD for investigation. SLCPD detectives immediately began securing and processing the scene and conducting initial witness interviews. The FBI opened a federal criminal civil rights investigation on August 11, 2014. Thereafter, federal and county authorities conducted cooperative, yet independent investigations into the shooting of Michael Brown.

1 The threshold determination that a case meets the standard for indictment rests with the prosecutor, *Wayte v. United States*, 470 U.S. 598, 607 (1985), and is "one of the most considered decisions a federal prosecutor makes." USAM 9-27.200, Annotation.

The encounter between Wilson and Brown took place over an approximately two-minute period of time at about noon on August 9, 2014. Wilson was on duty and driving his department-issued Chevy Tahoe SUV westbound on Canfield Drive in Ferguson, Missouri when he saw Brown and his friend, Witness 101, walking eastbound in the middle of the street. Brown and Witness 101 had just come from Ferguson Market and Liquor ("Ferguson Market"), a nearby convenience store, where, at approximately 11:53 a.m., Brown stole several packages of cigarillos. As captured on the store's surveillance video, when the store clerk tried to stop Brown, Brown used his physical size to stand over him and forcefully shove him away. As a result, an FPD dispatch call went out over the police radio for a "stealing in progress." The dispatch recordings and Wilson's radio transmissions establish that Wilson was aware of the theft and had a description of the suspects as he encountered Brown and Witness 101.

As Wilson drove toward Brown and Witness 101, he told the two men to walk on the sidewalk. According to Wilson's statement to prosecutors and investigators, he suspected that Brown and Witness 101 were involved in the incident at Ferguson Market based on the descriptions he heard on the radio and the cigarillos in Brown's hands. Wilson then called for backup, stating, "Put me on Canfield with two and send me another car." Wilson backed up his SUV and parked at an angle, blocking most of both lanes of traffic, and stopping Brown and Witness 101 from walking any further. Wilson attempted to open the driver's door of the SUV to exit his vehicle, but as he swung it open, the door came into contact with Brown's body and either rebounded closed or Brown pushed it closed.

Wilson and other witnesses stated that Brown then reached into the SUV through the open driver's window and punched and grabbed Wilson. This is corroborated by bruising on Wilson's jaw and scratches on his neck, the presence of Brown's DNA on Wilson's collar, shirt, and pants, and Wilson's DNA on Brown's palm. While there are other individuals who stated that Wilson reached out of the SUV and grabbed Brown by the neck, prosecutors could not credit their accounts because they were inconsistent with physical and forensic evidence, as detailed throughout this report.

Wilson told prosecutors and investigators that he responded to Brown reaching into the SUV and punching him by withdrawing his gun because he could not access less lethal weapons while seated inside the SUV. Brown then grabbed the weapon and struggled with Wilson to gain control of it. Wilson fired, striking Brown in the hand. Autopsy results and bullet trajectory, skin from Brown's palm on the outside of the SUV door as well as Brown's DNA on the inside of the driver's door corroborate Wilson's account that during the struggle, Brown used his right hand to grab and attempt to control Wilson's gun. According to three autopsies, Brown sustained a close range gunshot wound to the fleshy portion of his right hand at the base of his right thumb. Soot from the muzzle of the gun found embedded in the tissue of this wound coupled with indicia of thermal change from the heat of the muzzle indicate that Brown's hand was within inches of the muzzle of Wilson's gun when it was fired. The location of the recovered bullet in the side panel of the driver's door, just above Wilson's lap, also corroborates Wilson's account of the struggle over the gun and when the gun was fired, as do witness accounts that Wilson fired at least one shot from inside the SUV.

2 With the exception of Darren Wilson and Michael Brown, the names of individuals have been redacted as a safeguard against an invasion of their personal privacy.

Although no eyewitnesses directly corroborate Wilson's account of Brown's attempt to gain control of the gun, there is no credible evidence to disprove Wilson's account of what occurred inside the SUV. Some witnesses claim that Brown's arms were never inside the SUV. However, as discussed later in this report, those witness accounts could not be relied upon in a prosecution because credible witness accounts and physical and forensic evidence, *i.e.* Brown's

DNA inside the SUV and on Wilson's shirt collar and the bullet trajectory and close-range gunshot wound to Brown's hand, establish that Brown's arms and/or torso were inside the SUV.

After the initial shooting inside the SUV, the evidence establishes that Brown ran eastbound on Canfield Drive and Wilson chased after him. The autopsy results confirm that Wilson did not shoot Brown in the back as he was running away because there were no entrance wounds to Brown's back. The autopsy results alone do not indicate the direction Brown was facing when he received two wounds to his right arm, given the mobility of the arm. However, as detailed later in this report, there are no witness accounts that could be relied upon in a prosecution to prove that Wilson shot at Brown as he was running away. Witnesses who say so cannot be relied upon in a prosecution because they have given accounts that are inconsistent with the physical and forensic evidence or are significantly inconsistent with their own prior statements made throughout the investigation.

Brown ran at least 180 feet away from the SUV, as verified by the location of bloodstains on the roadway, which DNA analysis confirms was Brown's blood. Brown then turned around and came back toward Wilson, falling to his death approximately 21.6 feet west of the blood in the roadway. Those witness accounts stating that Brown never moved back toward Wilson could not be relied upon in a prosecution because their accounts cannot be reconciled with the DNA bloodstain evidence and other credible witness accounts.

As detailed throughout this report, several witnesses stated that Brown appeared to pose a physical threat to Wilson as he moved toward Wilson. According to these witnesses, who are corroborated by blood evidence in the roadway, as Brown continued to move toward Wilson, Wilson fired at Brown in what appeared to be self-defense and stopped firing once Brown fell to the ground. Wilson stated that he feared Brown would again assault him because of Brown's conduct at the SUV and because as Brown moved toward him, Wilson saw Brown reach his right hand under his t-shirt into what appeared to be his waistband. There is no evidence upon which prosecutors can rely to disprove Wilson's stated subjective belief that he feared for his safety.

Ballistics analysis indicates that Wilson fired a total of 12 shots, two from the SUV and ten on the roadway. Witness accounts and an audio recording indicate that when Wilson and Brown were on the roadway, Wilson fired three gunshot volleys, pausing in between each one. According to the autopsy results, Wilson shot and hit Brown as few as six or as many as eight times, including the gunshot to Brown's hand. Brown fell to the ground dead as a result of a gunshot to the apex of his head. With the exception of the first shot to Brown's hand, all of the shots that struck Brown were fired from a distance of more than two feet. As documented by crime scene photographs, Brown fell to the ground with his left, uninjured hand balled up by his waistband, and his right, injured hand palm up by his side. Witness accounts and cellular phone video prove that Wilson did not touch Brown's body after he fired the final shot and Brown fell to the ground.

Although there are several individuals who have stated that Brown held his hands up in an unambiguous sign of surrender prior to Wilson shooting him dead, their accounts do not support a prosecution of Wilson. As detailed throughout this report, some of those accounts are inaccurate because they are inconsistent with the physical and forensic evidence; some of those accounts are materially inconsistent with that witness's own prior statements with no explanation, credible for otherwise, as to why those accounts changed over time. Certain other witnesses who originally stated Brown had his hands up in surrender recanted their original accounts, admitting that they did not witness the shooting or parts of it, despite what they initially reported either to federal or local law enforcement or to the media. Prosecutors did not rely on those accounts when making a prosecutive decision.

While credible witnesses gave varying accounts of exactly what Brown was doing with his hands as he moved toward Wilson—*i.e.*, balling them, holding them out, or pulling up his pants up—and varying accounts of how he was moving—*i.e.*, "charging," moving in "slow motion," or "running"—they all establish that Brown was moving toward Wilson when Wilson shot him. Although some witnesses state that Brown held his hands up at shoulder level with his palms facing outward for a brief moment, these same witnesses describe Brown then dropping his hands and "charging" at Wilson.

By contrast, here is the summary from the DOJ's pattern-or-practice report. Read it closely and note that for all the official sounding language, it is remarkably vague. The legal statutes cited are only those that authorize the investigation, not the laws allegedly violated. The "unlawful" practices cited are not specified, nor are any legal decisions against Ferguson mentioned. Constitutional amendments are said to be violated, although that's a determination that can only be made by a judge, not by Justice Department lawyers. There are many references to their interviews with community members, "advocacy" groups, and others, but no explanation of process or procedure, or of evidentiary standards, because by the DOJ lawyers' own admission, those didn't apply.

I. REPORT SUMMARY

The Civil Rights Division of the United States Department of Justice opened its investigation of the Ferguson Police Department ("FPD") on September 4, 2014. This investigation was initiated under the pattern-or-practice provision of the Violent Crime Control and Law Enforcement Act of 1994, 42 U.S.C. § 14141, the Omnibus Crime Control and Safe Streets Act of 1968, 42 U.S.C. § 3789d ("Safe Streets Act"), and Title VI of the Civil Rights Act of 1964, 42 U.S.C. § 2000d ("Title VI"). This investigation has revealed a pattern or practice of unlawful conduct within the Ferguson Police Department that violates the First, Fourth, and Fourteenth Amendments to the United States Constitution, and federal statutory law.

Over the course of the investigation, we interviewed City officials, including City Manager John Shaw, Mayor James Knowles, Chief of Police Thomas Jackson, Municipal Judge Ronald Brockmeyer, the Municipal Court Clerk, Ferguson's Finance Director, half of FPD's sworn officers, and others. We spent, collectively, approximately 100 person-days onsite in Ferguson. We participated in ride-alongs with on-duty officers, reviewed over 35,000 pages of police records as well as thousands of emails and other electronic materials provided by the police department. Enlisting the assistance of statistical experts, we analyzed FPD's data on stops, searches, citations, and arrests, as well as data collected by the municipal court. We observed four separate sessions of Ferguson Municipal Court, interviewing dozens of people charged with local offenses, and we reviewed third-party studies regarding municipal court practices in Ferguson and St. Louis County more broadly. As in all of our investigations, we sought to engage the local community, conducting hundreds of in-person and telephone interviews of individuals who reside in Ferguson or who have had interactions with the police department. We contacted ten neighborhood associations and met with each group that responded to us, as well as several other community groups and advocacy organizations. Throughout the investigation, we relied on two police chiefs who accompanied us to Ferguson and who themselves interviewed City and police officials, spoke with community members, and reviewed FPD policies and incident reports.

We thank the City officials and the rank-and-file officers who have cooperated with this investigation and provided us with insights into the operation of the police department, including the municipal court. Notwithstanding our findings about Ferguson's approach to law enforcement and the policing culture it creates, we found many Ferguson police officers and other City employees to be dedicated public servants striving each day to perform their duties lawfully and with respect for all members of the Ferguson community. The importance of their often-selfless work cannot be overstated.

We are also grateful to the many members of the Ferguson community who have met with us to share their experiences. It became clear during our many conversations with Ferguson residents from throughout the City that many residents, black and white, genuinely embrace Ferguson's diversity and want to reemerge from the events of recent months a truly inclusive, united community. This

Report is intended to strengthen those efforts by recognizing the harms caused by Ferguson's law enforcement practices so that those harms can be better understood and overcome.

1 Ferguson's law enforcement practices are shaped by the City's focus on revenue rather than by public safety needs. This emphasis on revenue has compromised the institutional character of Ferguson's police department, contributing to a pattern of unconstitutional policing, and has also shaped its municipal court, leading to procedures that raise due process concerns and inflict unnecessary harm on members of the Ferguson community. Further, Ferguson's police and municipal court practices both reflect and exacerbate existing racial bias, including racial stereotypes. Ferguson's own data establish clear racial disparities that adversely impact African Americans. The evidence shows that discriminatory intent is part of the reason for these disparities. Over time, Ferguson's police and municipal court practices have sown deep mistrust between parts of the community and the police department, undermining law enforcement legitimacy among African Americans in particular.

I still look at this report and am unable to recognize the Ferguson in which I lived and worked. I see only a backwards, angry place that the Justice Department needed to create so that they could make a show of tearing it down. That Ferguson didn't exist, at least not in the time that I spent there. The most tragic effect of the DOJ's report is how it is likely to bring that terrible vision of a broken community one step closer to becoming reality.

Acknowledgments

I would like to pay tribute to the many, many members of the law enforcement community who came to Ferguson day after day to stand tall in the face of extreme violence and vitriolic hate speech, and who held their heads high while they were assaulted with bricks and fire and guns and bottles of urine. They are the heroes of Ferguson and I will never be able to thank them enough.

Thank you to my wife and children, my parents, brothers, sister, and extended family, who stood by me and gave me comfort during this painful chapter of my life.

Thank you to Colonel Al Eickhoff, Captain Rick Henke, Captain Dan DeCarli, Lieutenants Bill Ballard, Craig Rettke, and Ray Nabzdyk, Sergeants Harry Dilworth, Mike Wood, Tim Allen, Tim Harris, and Bill Mudd, and all the courageous members of the Ferguson Police Department.

Heartfelt gratitude to my friends and colleagues: Chief Kurt Frisz, Chief Jon Belmar, Colonels Ken Cox, Mike Dierkes, and Ken Gregory, Lieutenant Jim Vollmar, and the men and women of the Saint Louis County Police Department; Major Chuck Thal, the Missouri Police Chiefs Association, the St. Louis Area Police Chiefs Association and their member departments; the North County Municipal Police Chiefs Association and their member departments; all the federal agencies who gave their support during the unrest; Colonel Ron Replogle and the Missouri State Highway Patrol; and the Missouri National guard.

Thank you to the communications officers, corrections officers, clerks, and staff at Ferguson PD who stayed the course, and to Fire Chief Steve Rosenthal and the men and women of the Ferguson Fire Department, as well as the fire-fighters from other agencies who also faced violence while trying to keep Ferguson from burning.

Thank you to city attorney Stephanie Karr, city manager John Shaw, Mayor James Knowles III, city clerk Megan Asikainen, finance director Jeff Blume, and all the people at city hall and public works who stayed on the job and held the town together during dangerous times.

Much gratitude to Shannon Dandridge and the St. Louis Police Wives' Association, who gave food, shelter, and comfort to the brave officers, troopers, and guardsmen who braved the unrest and riots.

Thanks to my administrative assistant, Mary Simmons, who kept me centered and on task throughout those many weeks.

Thank you to Steve Heard, Dane Reid, Bob Aubuchon, Steve Anderson, Charles Glenn, and all my friends who defended and supported me during the troubles in Ferguson, including my Florissant family who gave me moments of refuge from the storm (you know who you are).

Special thanks to the good people of Ferguson who continue to believe in their city in the face of false witnesses; Chief Gregg Hall and the men and women of the Hazelwood Police Department; retired chief Carl Wolf, Dave Lommel and Drew Stewart from ITI; the Northwest Chamber of Commerce; and Sergeant Kevin Bernard and all the folks from the Billy Graham Rapid Response Team.

Thanks to the people of this country and the greater world, who took the time to send food and comfort, as well as letters and cards of thanks, support, encouragement, and prayer to my family, our police department, and officers within their own communities. I've heard stories like kids spending their allowances to bring pizza to their local police. I didn't get to respond to as many cards and letters as I wanted, but they filled walls in the break room for the officers to see.

I would also like to acknowledge and thank my coauthor and new friend, David Sobel, who guided me along the process of telling the story of this unique moment in American history. I am grateful not only for his skill but for his wisdom and advice. Many thanks, too, to my agent, Tom Miller of the Carol Mann Agency, for his vision and steadfast support.

Index